THE BUSY MAN'S
OLD TESTAMENT

DEDICATED

to all who have enough perseverance to read
through the Old Testament as condensed in the
passages chosen and the comments upon them.

The Busy Man's Old Testament

by

LESLIE D. WEATHERHEAD,

C.B.E., M.A., Ph.D., D.Litt., D.D.

Minister-Emeritus, The City Temple, London,
Formerly President of the Methodist Conference,
Past-President, The Institute of Religion and Medicine,
Hon. Chaplain to Her Majesty's Forces.

DENHOLM HOUSE PRESS
Robert Denholm House, Nutfield, Surrey

First published 1971

© *1971 Leslie D. Weatherhead*

ISBN 0 85213 038 4

Published simultaneously in the U.S.A.
by Abingdon Press.

BOOKS BY REV. LESLIE D. WEATHERHEAD, C.B.E.,
M.A., Ph.D., D.Litt., D.D.

Published by Denholm House Press

Life Begins at Death   The Busy Man's Old Testament

Published by the Epworth Press
The Transforming Friendship   The Resurrection and the Life
Psychology in the Service of   That Immortal Sea
   the Soul   Over his own Signature
The Will of God   Jesus and Ourselves
Salute to a Sufferer

Published by Hodder and Stoughton
Psychology, Religion and Healing   When the Lamp Flickers
His Life and Ours   Prescription for Anxiety
How can I find God?   A Private House of Prayer
Psychology and Life   Key next Door
It happened in Palestine   Wounded Spirits
A Shepherd Remembers   The Christian Agnostic
Personalities of the Passion   The Resurrection of Christ
In Quest of a Kingdom

Published in Fontana Books
A Plain Man looks at the Cross

Published by the Student Christian Movement Press
Why do men Suffer?   Discipleship
The Mastery of Sex through Psychology and Religion

Printed by COX AND WYMAN LTD.,
London, Reading and Fakenham

INTRODUCTION

The aim of this book is to persuade people to read their Bibles. There is probably a Bible in almost every home in Britain. Yet it must be the least read of all the best sellers in the world. Any new translations are snapped up at once showing a real hunger for truth about God. In 1961 the New Testament of the New English Bible was published. Seven million copies have been sold. Yet few turn to the Bible frequently, especially the Old Testament.

It *used* to be produced unattractively, in parallel columns and small print, but this is not now a reason for its lying unread. The answer is that the Old Testament is such a mixture of the valuable and the valueless, the deeply moving and that which fails to touch our lives at any point.

In the Old Testament there is much that leaves us cold, e.g., regulations for priests in Leviticus, and some of the visions of Ezekiel. Some of it affronts us as sub-Christian—e.g. Saul being told to smite the Amalekites and kill the women and children and even the animals (1 Samuel 15: 3), or the dashing of babies against rocks (Psalm 137: 8–9). Some of it is apparently written in a code to which we have lost the key, and some of it doesn't make any sense at all. We feel that these passages do not contain for us "the Word of God".

My aim is to provide the busy man with the richness the Old Testament contains, while avoiding matter which is not relevant to his need. I wish it were possible to quote the worthwhile passages in full, but this would make too big and bulky a volume. So a Bible must be available as well as this book. References are thus constantly made. The book is constructed for those who want to "read the Bible right through", but who don't want in the process to miss the unity of its great themes.

The references refer to the parts of the book which are well worth reading and pondering, with copious comments to make the meaning and present-day relevance of the text a bit clearer. I would like the reader who perseveres to the end to feel that he has read through the Old Testament in so far as it has a message for him in the twentieth century.

During the writing of this book the Old Testament portion of the New English Bible was published. It lights up many dark places and is recommended to be used with this book.

This book is not written for ministers, let alone scholars, but for the ordinary man in the pew, or even the street. If he reads as directed, namely, the passages in heavy type, the author believes that he will not miss much in the Old Testament that is of devotional value for the busy man of today.

I should like to add a special word of gratitude to my friend the Rev. Paul Morton-George, M.A., who has not only read through the manuscript and made helpful suggestions, but, at my request, has added material of his own which has greatly enhanced the value of the book.

I must thank my secretary, Miss Elsie Thompson, for her help in typing the manuscript and correcting the proofs.

LESLIE D. WEATHERHEAD.

BEXHILL-ON-SEA,
SUSSEX.
1970.

CONTENTS

Bible references printed in heavy type are the author's selections for reading.

Passages in italics are

(a) Introduction and background to the book in question, or

(b) Linking comments on Bible material not recommended for reading.

Quotations from the Bible are from the Authorised Version, unless otherwise stated.

GENESIS

Remember at the outset that the book of Genesis is not the work of one writer but contains many strands gathered from many ancient sources going back hundreds of years B.C. The editor regarded each as too sacred to be altered, so he included them as they were, with what we might call the paste pot and scissors method. Hence the occasional differences and apparent contradictions.

Genesis 1: 1—2: 3

Modern scientists still debate *how* our universe came in to being. This editor is much more concerned with *why* it did. He has no idea of writing accurate science. He offers a parable of Creation in order to portray God on whom depends the creation of the universe, and who created man to be the crown of creation and his own vice regent.

Chapter 2 : 4 begins a second and probably earlier form of this parable of the creation of man and woman.

Genesis 2: 18—3: 24

Here is the famous allegory of the creation of man and of woman from man, "bone of (his) bones and flesh of (his) flesh", and the prophecy that a man will leave his parents' home, cleave to his wife and "they shall be one flesh". Jesus himself quoted this as the permanent basis of marriage—the union of two personalities.

Serpents from ancient times have been eminent for their cleverness ("wise as serpents" Matthew 10: 16) and here we see evil in cunning form entering a situation previously pure bliss and making it sordid and "nasty". Here is the birth of shame which has persisted until the present day.

In short, in a world God intended to be Paradise, evil has somehow found entrance with disastrous results. How did the serpent get into the garden? How did it elude the guardian angel? Why is it allowed such power over men? We are not told. But evil is portrayed as the devil or devils, or some evil energy hostile to God's will which he will finally deal with triumphantly.

Genesis 4: 1–16

In this story of Cain and Abel it is now assumed that the earth has a population so that the story belongs to a later period and the question, "Who was Cain's wife?" falls to the ground, though it never could have arisen if the Adam and Eve story had been taken as the parable which it is.

Murder took place and the widely held belief was expressed that "blood cried from the ground" for vengeance. God sets a mark on Cain not to brand him as a murderer but mercifully to stop anyone else shedding blood by killing him, and starting a blood feud. Here the question first finds expression which we must still ask, "Am I my brother's keeper?" Murder is righly regarded as a terrible wrong. Yet God's mercy is shown here extending even to one who commits it. This is a remarkable anticipation of God's attitude to sinners as Jesus was much later to reveal it. So far from leaving them to their own devices, God sets out to "seek and save that which was lost".

Genesis 6: 5—7: 24

Here we have a typical mixture of legend and fact drawn from many sources, mainly Babylonian, deriving originally from some flood disaster of vast proportions, in which much damage was done and many lost their lives. It could not, of course, have covered the whole earth as we now know it.

Similar flood stories occur in the literature of other civilisations. It is possible that Noah and his family saw the rising waters in time to build some kind of boat. The idea of the animals going in "two by two" was a picturesque way of accounting for the continuity of animal life. The idea that God "repented" of His creation because man turned out so badly shows that the writer thinks of God as reacting in the way he himself would have done.

Later God is believed to promise, "While the earth remaineth, seedtime and harvest, and cold and heat, and summer and winter, and day and night shall not cease." (8 : 22). In 9 : 5–6 are the words which were the basis for the old argument for capital punishment.

Genesis 9: 8–17

Here is the idea that the rainbow was the token of God's covenant that never again would water destroy "all flesh" (verse 15). Today we know *how* a rainbow comes into existence, but its beauty can still speak to us of the God of Beauty and of his mercy toward mankind.

Genesis 11: 1–9

Here we read primitive man's "explanation" of how different nations came to speak in different tongues, and the vain attempt of man to retain the one language which it was supposed existed in the beginning. That this was never so, of course, is proved in many ways, including inscriptions found all over the world pre-dating the Babel story.

Just as God is portrayed as driving Adam and Eve from the garden lest they know too much, so he is conceived here as confounding their language into many tongues for fear of what a united humanity might achieve.

The tower would be a Zikkurat, a kind of pyramid rising in terraces with a temple at the top giving access to heaven, but the builders gave up before completing the tower—the Lord "scattered them abroad" (verse 8).

The ancient sense of need for a common language has survived to our own time. It is felt in international contacts and conferences in many spheres. But deeper still is the need to understand not just the words but the ideas of other men. We need to "speak one another's language".

Genesis 12: 1–9; 13: 1–4

In this story of the Call of Abraham God's purpose in the original act of Creation is taken a step further. The response of Abraham to the call is still thrilling to read. He leaves the familiar and the known, staking everything on what he believes to be God's promise to bless him and see him through all the dangers and uncertainties of life in a new land. Jesus spoke of Zaccheus as "a son of Abraham" (Luke 19: 9) because he showed the same trust and confidence in God. Here, too, is the first hint of a nation to be born which God will use in a special way.

He arrives at Bethel and builds an altar. Remembering this heroic adventure of faith, one sings with new significance the hymn:

O God of Bethel by whose hand Thy people still are fed.

Many have wondered why the reference to "Bethel". The experience of Abraham thousands of years ago makes it clear, especially when we include the experience of Jacob at Bethel (28: 19 ff. p. 16). The setting up of a stone is interesting and occurs frequently in the Old Testament. It was then widely believed that a stone could be inhabited by a deity.

We may pass over the separation of Abraham and Lot. The land is not rich enough for the herds of both; Abraham generously lets Lot choose, and he chooses the rich Jordan valley, leaving Abraham Canaan. Lot got into trouble and had to be rescued (chapter 14). The story of his wife being made into a pillar of salt was probably invented by the inspection of a mound of vaguely human shape encrusted with salt from the Dead Sea. Such "pillars of salt" are still to be found.

Abraham, desperate for an heir (how else was he to be the founder of a great nation, as God had promised?), has intercourse at his wife's suggestion with Hagar, her maid. She bears Ishmael, the father of the Arab nation, of whom it was said, "his hand will be against every man, and every man's hand against him" (16: 12).

12

Genesis 17: 15—18: 14

God promises that Abraham shall have a son by Sarah, his wife, and shall be the father of many who shall all be circumcised as a sign that they belong to the true family (17: 11). Subsequently all males circumcised after eight days were within the covenant made with Jehovah. This idea of a covenant between God and the nation will recur again and again as we read on.

Genesis 21: 1–7; 22: 1–19

No modern reader should miss this sublime story beautifully told of Abraham's devotion to God, making him willing to sacrifice his only son, begotten with such difficulty, and on whose survival so much depended, because he believed God asked it of him. A great depth of pathos is reached in Isaac's question in Chapter 22, verse 7, and in Abraham's sublime reply in verse 8.

> *All for sin could not atone;*
> *Thou must save, and Thou alone.*

This is how Toplady, an 18th-century hymn writer, was to sum it up. It is said that after this incident men no longer offered their sons, but substituted rams in the Temple as blood-sacrifices. Israel learned only very slowly that there were offerings even more precious than the blood of sheep and goats (Psalm 51: 16; Micah 6: 6–8). Of course Isaac must be spared or how are Abraham's descendants to multiply since Isaac was the only legitimate son?

Genesis 24: 1–48

We pass over the death and burial of Sarah, Abraham's wife and Isaac's mother, and read now the story of a choice of wife for Isaac. She must not be a foreigner. The method is strange to us today but is fascinatingly told in the text. Laban, Rebekah's father, accepts the offer of marriage as of God's guidance. Isaac accepts the bride and Abraham dies happy (25: 8). The continuance of his family and their destiny to become a great nation seems assured.

Main Biblical events and the Old Testament books which are linked with them

(Most dates are approximate)

	Date B.C.	Book
Creation		Genesis
The Flood		Genesis
Migration under Abraham	1650	Genesis
Isaac and Jacob	1600–1500	Genesis
Joseph's exile and rise to power	14th Century	Genesis
The Exodus under Moses	13th Century	Exodus
The Wilderness journeys	13th Century	Exodus
Conquest of Canaan	1220 and following years	Joshua
The times of the Judges	1200–1020	Judges*
		Ruth*
Samuel, priest and prophet		I Samuel
Beginning of Monarchy	1020	I Samuel
Reign of David	1004–961	II Samuel
		I Chronicles
Reign of Solomon	961–922	I Kings 1–11
		II Chronicles 1–9
The Divided Kingdom	922–586	I Kings 12—II Kings 25
		II Chronicles 10–36
		Hosea
		Amos
		Zephaniah
Fall of Samaria	723–2	II Kings 18: 9–12
End of Northern Kingdom }		Jonah*
The Southern Kingdom continues alone		Isaiah 1–39

Event	Date	Books
Finding of the Law Book }	621	Deuteronomy
Reforms of Josiah	612	Nahum
Fall of Nineveh to the Babylonians	597	Ezekiel
First deportation of Jews to Babylon }		II Kings 25
Fall of Jerusalem }	586	Jeremiah
End of Southern Kingdom }		Obadiah
		Isaiah 40–55
		Daniel*
Exile in Babylon	586–538	
Capture of Babylon by Cyrus of Persia	539	Ezra 1
Edict of Cyrus for return of exiles	538	Ezra 1
First return of exiles to Palestine	537	Ezra and Nehemiah
Various groups of exiles return	537–390	Jonah†
		Isaiah 56–66
Re-building of Temple begins	520	Haggai
		Zechariah
		Malachi
		Esther*
	460	
Nehemiah comes to Jerusalem	444	Nehemiah
Ezra comes to Jerusalem	397	Ezra/Nehemiah
	4th century	Ruth†
		Job
		Joel
Conquest of Palestine by Alexander the Great of Greece	332	Habakkuk
Persecution of Jews by Antiochus Epiphanes of Greece	168	Daniel†
Maccabean revolt against Antiochus	167	Esther†
	150	

*† Books indicated thus have contents linked with historical periods or events (marked by *) but were written to serve the special needs of another period (marked †).

15

Genesis 25: 19–34

After the account of the birth of Esau and Jacob comes the well-known story of the mess of pottage.

Esau was the "out of doors" boy who loved hunting and delighted his father with the game he brought home. Jacob was the quiet "home boy", but Esau, the senior by only a moment, sold his birthright for a tasty stew when he was faint with hunger after hunting.

Genesis 27: 1–41

This is well worth attention, showing how in ancient times a blessing was an important thing that could not—as it were—be taken back. Even when Isaac knows he has been deceived by the cunning plot devised by his wife and his son Jacob, the latter still gets away with the blessing, and Esau has to put up with a very poor substitute and hates Jacob with murderous intent (verse 41).

Genesis 28: 10—29: 1

You can still find the place where Jacob slept opposite a steep hillside, terraced so that it could be cultivated, and still looking like a grand staircase leading to the stars. No wonder, then, that a stairway, not a ladder, formed what we should now call the "manifest content", i.e. the stage scenery of his dream. It was widely believed that in sleep the deities could visit men and guide and advise them. When he awakens, the awe of a Divine Presence is still with him (verses 16, 17). Then he makes his bargain that if God will take care of him he will give God ten per cent of his income and an altar. The crafty cheat seems by the dream to be a cleansed and new man, and, as the future shows, becomes one of the most important men in the Bible.

Genesis 29: 1–30

This is the account of how Jacob the deceiver is deceived. Jacob, on his journey, comes to a well and falls in love at sight with Rachel, daughter of Laban, his uncle, who is keeping her father's sheep. Laban welcomes his nephew, but the latter has no money, no "bride-price" to offer, so Laban accepts in return the suggestion that Jacob works without pay for seven years. This Jacob does "and they seemed unto him but a few days, for the love he had to her" (verse 20).

Subsequently, by a deception hard to understand, Laban fobs Jacob off with his elder daughter, Leah, the weak (? watery) eyed elder girl and demands another seven years' service for Rachel.

But alas, Rachel was barren and the "tribes of Israel" were born of Leah and Rachel's handmaid Bilhah, and then Leah's maid Zilpah. Finally Rachel had a son by Jacob and he became the famous Joseph.

Jacob, having quarrelled with Laban, returned to the land of Canaan (31: 18), and when overtaken and charged, Jacob made a covenant with Laban and raised another stone called Mizpah, and said, "The Lord watch between me and thee, when we are absent one from another." I still have a gold ring given me by my mother on which the word "Mizpah" is engraved. So Jacob and Laban parted and Jacob went on his way.

Genesis 32: 22–32

Jacob makes it up with Esau and there follows the strange experience of his wrestling all night with an angel. Read Charles Wesley's great hymn, "Come O Thou traveller unknown". In eastern thought to know a person's name is to have power over them. In some eastern countries the bride will not give her true name to her betrothed until after the ceremony when he alone has power over her. Mohammedan soldiers serving in the First World War would frequently refuse to give their true names. Jesus dealing with the demented man among the tombs demands to know the patient's name. The patient would thus recognise that Jesus was seeking power over him for his good and he replied, "My name is Legion," a reference, perhaps, to the Roman Legion which had terrified him in his childhood. So in this story of some great spiritual experience the angel learns Jacob's name, but Jacob never learns that of the angel (verse 29). Jacob gets a new name, ISRAEL. This is the first emergence in literature of this word, now in the papers every day. It can mean "He who striveth with God". "Thou hast striven with God," says the angel, "and prevailed" (verse 28). Jacob calls the place "Peniel" which means "the face of God".

It is a strange experience and hard to fit into modern thought. Each stream—in this case the Jabbok—had its controlling spirit or genie which often resisted those who crossed its stream. Spirits must depart before daybreak. Hence Wesley's couplet:

> *With Thee all night I mean to stay*
> *And wrestle till the break of day.*

But for Jacob this was no hostile spirit but one who came from God and fought in such a material way that Jacob's thigh was put out of joint. Was the stream in flood? Did Jacob slip on a slippery stone in the dark and slip a disc or dislocate his hip? We cannot be sure, but the writer of the day put it all down to wrestling with an "angel" whose blessing and goodwill were sought. Certainly to Jacob himself it was a rich, spiritual experience, "I have seen God face to face," and he went on blessed and enheartened.

Jacob makes it up with Esau and goes to Shechem and thence, after a terrible revenge for ill done to Dinah, his sister, Jacob goes to Bethel. Here Rachel dies in giving birth to Benjamin.

Genesis 37: 1–36

Joseph, his father's pet (verse 3), is hated for that reason by his brethren and their hatred pushes him down into inferiority. In the dream therefore the compensation-wish is expressed. The sheaf is the symbol of fertility, the stars of power. To all Nomadic tribes the begetting of a multitude of offspring is the most satisfactory means of securing wealth and power. Obviously it is no use having wealth if a neighbouring tribe by force of superior numbers could vanquish the wealthy tribe whenever it liked. We remember how the promise came to Abraham that his seed should be as the sand on the seashore for *multitude*. The little herd-boy fulfils his wish in a dream in which he founds a family greater and wealthier than that of his older brethren. The interpretation of the dream is the wish for power, and compensation for the unrealised desires of youth. It was to prove more than a dream, as we shall see.

Joseph escapes the murderous plot of his brothers through the kindness of the eldest, Reuben, and arrives in Egypt where he prospers but is falsely accused of adultery with his master's wife who has tried to seduce him. When he refused, she charges him with attempted rape and he is imprisoned. In prison he encounters a butler and baker, rightly interprets their dreams and subsequently those of Pharaoh. These warn Pharaoh of famine and Joseph organises the storage of supplies against the famine to come. Pharaoh therefore restores Joseph to power.

Genesis 42—46: 7

This is a thrilling story that needs little comment. It could be summarised by a verse further on (50: 20) where Joseph says to his brothers, "Ye thought evil against me; but God meant it unto good". It is a pre-glimpse of St. Paul's great affirmation in Romans 8: 28, "To those who love God, . . . everything that happens fits into a pattern for good" (Phillips). But as with Joseph, the hard times have to be lived through in trust before they are seen in perspective, and God's good purpose, worked out in spite of them and through them, becomes plain.

So the Israelites get into Egypt (47: 27) *or rather the adjoining Goshen, but they become serfs. Jacob extracts an oath that Joseph will see that he is buried in Canaan and blesses the two sons of Joseph, Ephraim and Manasseh, who found independent tribes.*

Genesis 50: 1–26

The book of Genesis closes with the death of Jacob and his burial, by Pharaoh's consent, in the land of Canaan in the cave of Machpelah. Joseph re-affirms his forgiveness of his brothers and adds the sentence we have quoted above

(50:20–21). Finally Joseph, having foretold that the Israelites will be brought out of Egypt (50: 24) dies himself and is embalmed and buried in Egypt. The date is about 1500 B.C. and the scene moves to Egypt where "there arose up a new king over Egypt, which knew not Joseph" (Exodus 1: 8). The divine promise to Abraham that his decendants would form a nation blessed by God seems very far from fulfilment.

EXODUS

This book contains the epic story of Moses' leadership in guiding the children of Israel toward the "Promised Land" of Canaan. Only about seventy entered Egypt but they were there so long (one estimate is 430 years), that the people who went into the wilderness numbered possibly several thousand. This exodus was the key event in their history. It took place in the 13th century B.C. It changed them from a rabble of slaves into a nation. The phrase used about God in the Old Testament more than any other is that "he brought them up out of Egypt". This showed clearly that the patriarchs from Abraham to Joseph had been right. God had a purpose for this people. Through success and failure, loyalty and unfaithfulness, they were to learn what that purpose was.

Exodus 1: 8—2: 22
The familiar story of the birth and youth of Moses never fails to stir us, with its account of one family's successful resistance to a ruthless ruler.

Exodus 3: 1–18
The burning bush story may make the modern man dubious, but I have read of a bush found in that area which developed berries which, when ripe, contained an inflammable gas. When the heat of the sun made these berries burst the whole bush would be a burning mass until the gas was burnt off.

The leaves and twigs would not be ignited and the blaze would last only a few minutes. Naturally, to Moses, the sight of a bush burning but not consumed became a religious experience just as a perfectly natural event—the rainbow—had a religious content to his predecessors.

The title "I am that I am" became much clearer to me when the late Prof. J. A. Findlay translated it, "I will be what I always have been"—in other words, "You can depend on me". The title thus means, "The Dependable One".

We can omit the early part of Chapter 4. Moses wants to withdraw from the leadership on account of his being a poor speaker, but God promises to be with him and to use the more eloquent Aaron. Moses does, however, return to Egypt to plead with Pharaoh to let the people go.

Exodus 5

The children of Israel have been useful slaves to the Egyptians so Pharaoh is loath to let them go. Pharaoh not only refuses, but takes steps to make their slavery more intolerable, denying them even the straw they needed to make bricks (verse 7), and yet demanding that the number of bricks is not diminished. Moses taxes God with these things. Old Testament characters did not hesitate to complain to God in their prayers, when they felt badly done by! (verses 22–3).

Exodus 7: 14–25

Moses now threatens Pharaoh with plagues if he will not let the Israelites depart.

It may be that the period under discussion coincided with a cosmic disturbance caused by the earth passing through the dusty tail of a large comet. About this comet Servius wrote: "It was not a flaming but a bloody redness. A fine dust of rusty colour gave a bloody colouring to all water." Hence the "rivers of blood". A similar occurrence is said to have taken place in Mexico, "when the earth quaked and the sun's motion was interrupted and the water in the rivers turned to blood". The dust irritated the skin of men and cattle causing boils in men and the "murrain" in the cattle.

The Finns have a similar story in their ancient books. The Red Sea may have acquired its name from this dust which darkened the sunlight and, as it cleared, the moon still looked like blood. The Israelites were so certain that God was thus working for them that Joel (Joel 2: 28–32) prophesies "the sun shall be turned into darkness and the moon into blood"—a prophecy repeated by Peter on the day of Pentecost (Acts 2: 19–20). It seemed that supernatural activity having been once accompanied by these cosmic disturbances, they would be repeated again whenever God intervened to help his people. The evidence for this cosmic disturbance is set out in Velikovsky's great book, "Worlds in Collision".[1]

There follows a sequence of horrors. Plagues of frogs, lice, mosquitoes, flies, the murrain on all the animals (the word for cattle includes all domestic animals, such as camels and donkeys), boils and blains, so-called Nile scab of irritating red blisters on the skin, hail, locusts, a "thick darkness" and so on. (10: 22. See Worlds in Collision, *p.* 69) *The ancient book of the Finns* (Kalevala) *tells of a time when "hailstones of iron fell from the sky" and the sun and moon "were stolen from the sky".*

Evidently some terrifying event took place and rabbinical tradition, contradicting the Bible story, says that thousands of Israelites perished also and only a fraction survived to leave Egypt. Whatever did happen has been woven into the story to show God's special protection of the Israelites, the peak of the story being the deaths of the first-born of Egypt and the final deliverance of Israel.

Many people still interpret events in this way. A modern example is the calm sea at the evacuation of Allied troops from Dunkirk in 1940. *This was believed to be providential. Is this interpretation right? If it means that God has "favourites"* (Israel, the Allies) *it is false, because he is no respecter of persons. If it means that God wove this event into his purpose* (to make Israel a nation, to overthrow Nazism) *then it is not unreasonable.*

Exodus 12: 1–36

These verses are important because they give—however

[1] Gollancz, 1960.

mixed with folklore—the story of the first institution of the Passover—a feast that has continued to this day. Jesus called the last supper "this Passover" which he so desired to celebrate with his men before the Crucifixion (Mark 14: 12). Blood sprinkled on the door posts of a Hebrew home assured the inmates that they were safe. The angel of destruction would "pass over" the house so betokened and death would fall only on Egypt's first-born and on their cattle. No wonder "there was a great cry in Egypt for there was not a house where there was not one dead" (12: 30).

It is impossible to harmonise in our minds this story of cruelty and favouritism (though Goshen, where the Israelites lived, was a somewhat isolated part of Egypt) with what Jesus told us about God, but one fact emerges, that the power of Egypt over Israel was broken and a vast concourse of people set out with flocks and herds for the Promised Land. Flinders Petrie suggested that the word for "family" has been mistranslated "thousand" and that the number that set out was six hundred families. This is a figure which makes the exodus more believable.

The people of Israel never forgot their escape from the house of bondage in Egypt, though many must have been left behind. When people come safely through some disaster, they often feel that "there must have been a purpose in it". Similarly the Exodus remained for all time a sign to Israel that God had a purpose for them, as Abraham had foreseen.

Exodus 13: 17–22
So the pilgrimage began with a censer carried in front symbolising the presence of God, lest people thought he was left behind in Egypt, and was limited to a locality like the gods of Egypt. The smoke of the censer was like a pillar of cloud by day and, when the smoke was lit up by the fire of the censer, it looked at night like a pillar of fire. Many people today are helped by having, for example, in churches, things which symbolise the unseen presence of God.

Exodus 14: 1–31
We may remember that one arm of the Red Sea contained

lagoons like a necklace joined by water only at high tide and separated at low tide by dry land. The Israelites, guided by the brilliant generalship of Moses, crossed when the tide was low and the east wind strong, but the unfortunate Egyptians, pursuing them with heavy iron chariots, got stuck in the mud and subsequently were engulfed by the returning tide. No wonder "the people . . . believed the Lord, and his servant Moses" (verse 31).

Exodus 15: 27—16: 21

So Moses brought them "from the Red sea" (15: 22) and dealt with their problems of undrinkable water and their murmurings over their diet, teaching them to use the dew and the quails.

J. A. Findlay tells us that every September flocks of quails blow in from Cyprus over Gaza and into the wilderness. The people of Gaza throw down their tools and catch them in nets as they fall, wearied from their long flight over the sea, and the markets of Jerusalem are glutted with them. Travellers have also told of seeing the sand of the desert covered with what looked like little round, white balls which melt in the sun but are sweet and sustaining. The Arabs still call them "manna". The monks at the famous monastery on Mt. Sinai still gather them and say it is the gum that falls from the tamarisk bushes. It must be picked up quickly or it disappears. No wonder the Israelites called it "man-hu" (What is it?) and thought of it as specially sent by God from heaven for their delectation—"the taste of it was like wafers made with honey" (16: 31). They tended to cling to the idea, which we have seen (p. 23) to be mistaken, that they were God's "favourites".

We pass over the story of Moses striking a rock to obtain water for the mutinous people—a story not very strange to a modern dowser— and of his assistance to Joshua—who emerges as a military leader against Amalek—by keeping his hands raised in supplication to God, assisted by Aaron and Hur who "stayed up his hands" one on either side (17: 12). Jethro, Moses' father-in-law, sees that the task of

Moses in being continually beset to solve problems of people who sought his advice is too much for him (18: 18) and suggests the creation of a panel of "judges" to hear complaints and settle disputes. Moses does this and only hears cases the judges feel beyond them. They come to Sinai which then was an active volcano.

Exodus 19: 1—20: 21

Though we may find it hard to believe that long life can be assured by honouring one's parents (20: 12), the famous Ten Commandments are remarkably up to date. We must be also impressed by the brilliant strategy of Moses. He knew the laws of Hammurabi the Babylonian King at an earlier date and Moses edited them as rules the Israelites should keep if their health, physical, moral, mental and spiritual were to be maintained. He was convinced that they represented God's will for Israel and so he got the sanction of the terrifying deity who lived among the smoke and fire of Sinai, then an active volcano some 7,000 feet high. Even touching the mountain could bring the death-penalty (19: 12). What could the people do but promise to keep rules given them under such awe-ful circumstances accompanied by such terrible penalties for disobedience? They have been the basis of morality ever since.[1]

Exodus 25: 10—26: 1

The ark plays such a large part in the adventures of Israel that it is important to know about its origin. It was the supreme symbol of the presence of God. The phrase "the mercy seat" is still heard and we should know what it refers to. The same applies to references to the "tabernacle" but there is no need to go into the minute details about it or about the court in which it was housed, or of Aaron's vestments and the sacrifices to be made on the altar.

Exodus 32: 1—33: 11

In Moses' absence Aaron incites the people to make a

[1] See *Smoke on the Mountain—an Interpretation of the Ten Commandments in terms of today* by Joy Davidman. (Hodder and Stoughton, 1955) with a preface by C. S. Lewis.

golden calf from their golden ornaments pretending that this was the god who brought them out of Egypt (verse 4). Moses retaliates in great anger and destroys the calf (verse 20), and utters the great challenge, "Who is on the Lord's side?" (verse 26). There follows the story of a great purge when many die.

Why was Moses so incensed? The Israelites were shortly to settle in a land where many idols were worshipped as gods. It would be all too easy to slip away from faith in one God alone and to be absorbed into the religion of the land. This was in fact to happen again and again in their history. So when Aaron himself encouraged that early apostasy, Moses put the whole weight of his authority against it.

Moses shows his greatness by offering to be blotted out of God's book if the sin of the people is beyond the divine forgiveness (verses 31–32), but God reassures Moses who continues to lead the people towards the Promised Land. "The Lord spake unto Moses face to face, as a man speaketh unto his friend" (33: 11).

We have to remember that at this time God was a remote figure to most people and they thought of him as related to the nation rather than to individuals within it. So here is a significant sign of the growth of personal religion. This eventually found its fulfilment in the teaching of Jesus.

Exodus 33: 12—34: 8
Moses seeks a closer relationship with God and is assured of the divine presence (verse 14) and God, in a folk-lore type of story, shows Moses his back. No one is to see God's face and live. Moses is told to prepare tables of stone and on them to write the instructions which God will give him (34: 1).

Exodus 34: 29–35
Moses' face is transfigured by his fellowship with God and everybody notices it. There follows some repetition of the commandments here and a vast amount of directions regarding the tabernacle and the dedication of Aaron to the priesthood.

LEVITICUS

This book concerns itself with the minutiae of the sacrifices on the altar and the sins which demanded such sacrifices. For devotional purposes, it may be omitted altogether.

Chapter 7: 22 ff. gives us the origin of eating kosher meat, which is of interest to those of us with Jewish friends, and 16: 8–26 gives us the strange story of the scapegoat on to whose innocent head the iniquities of men could be heaped before the animal was driven into the wilderness to die. Hence the meaning of the word in everyday speech today. Here is the germ idea that an animal's life could bear the sin of men. Cf. "Behold the Lamb of God" (John 1: 35). We noticed earlier (p. 15) how Abraham realised that only God himself could provide a sacrifice adequate for that.

Note the emphasis on morality, not just because communal life demanded it but because God, the God who had delivered them from Egypt, required it. Unlike the religions around them, to the Jew to be religious was to be moral, honest and straightforward in business and in private life. *Their* God was *holy* and demanded holiness from his worshippers. The link between morality and religion, which is widely questioned today, is strongly upheld in the Bible.

The consecration of priests, the forbidden degrees of marriage, what constituted ritual uncleanness, these matters are no longer of interest to the busy man of today.

We can admire the efforts made to combat disease and to prevent the spread of infection, but we find little in Leviticus with which to feed our souls. There is only an odd bit of interest here and there, e.g. the origin of tithes, or giving one tenth of one's substance to God (27: 30) which we noticed first in Jacob (Genesis 28: 22), and the idea that blood meant life and the sacrifice of an animal symbolised men giving life itself, in order to be reconciled with God.

This throws light on the many references to "blood" in other parts of the Bible, including the New Testament and, later, in Christian hymns.

NUMBERS

This book derives its name from the census made of the various tribes of Israel. Perhaps (as we noted on p. 24) the word for "thousand" should be translated "family" (1 : 47). Six hundred families would be care enough!

The book could more accurately be called "the wilderness experience" for it describes, four hundred years after they happened, the events which for a whole generation and more took place as the Israelites moved through the desert east of the Dead Sea and the Jordan—since the more direct western route had been blocked by powerful enemies—on their way to the "Promised Land".

It cannot be called history in our sense, so composite is its authorship and so distant from the events themselves, but a certain amount of valuable narrative comes through and the religious ideas of the period in which it was written—perhaps the fifth century B.C.—are of interest, as is the background of nomadic life in the desert.

Moses is still the dominating personality of this book, and the whole civilised world even now owes him an unpayable debt for his insistence on the moral principles which he introduced in the Ten Commandments and elsewhere. Law was based on religion. It was God's law and must be kept. The whole of life—in every aspect—was God-centred. God mattered supremely in every activity of man.

Our idea of the omnipresence of God was slow to take root in the minds of the people, and his presence was still centred in the Ark about which we hear much in Numbers, but this focussing of the divine Presence in the Ark created the spirit of worship and reverence which teaching about an omnipresent deity could not, at that stage, have established.[1]

We become aware of the greatness of Moses, his devotion to God, his devotion to the people committed to his charge and his training of men who will be ready to fight the battles that will follow.

Numbers 6: 1–5
This shows the origin of the Nazarites, to which John the Baptist belonged. But their rules are not binding on the modern Christian, any more than upon people of those days who did not undertake the Nazarite vows. Moreover, the vow was for a period only (6: 13).

Numbers 6: 23–27
One of the most beautiful blessings in the Bible. We can still meaningfully use this gem which goes back literally thousands of years.

Numbers 9: 1–5
The order to keep the Passover is still obeyed, since it signalled the all-important Exodus.

We omit the sedition of Miriam and Aaron with Miriam's punishment of leprosy (the word leprosy covered almost any skin disease and hers may have been a hysterical rash), the report of the spies who bring back fruit which proves what a different country from the bare desert lies ahead, and the grumbling of the people which so upset Moses.

Numbers 15: 32–36
Note the ancient attitude to one who broke the sabbath and compare it with the permissiveness of today. Neither extreme reflects the teaching of Jesus. He rejected rigid unalterable rules, but he honoured the day as God's gift to man of one day in seven which is different. If we erect no safeguards at all, there will eventually be nothing to protect.

[1] See Numbers 10: 29–36.

The elevation of a brazen serpent (21: 5–9) *suggests to the modern man the power of mind over body. I have pointed out elsewhere[1] that Jesus himself used suggestion in some of the cures he carried out. But still more important is the use which Jesus makes of this incident (John 3: 13–15) to illustrate the response of faith in him which could give people new (eternal) life.*

One of the strange stories is that of Balaam and his talking ass. A heathen prophet declares that nothing can prevent God's people following God's guidance and even the donkey agrees.

A plague curses the people (25: 9), *but Moses, Caleb and Joshua are untouched, and the book closes with the appointment of Joshua as Moses' successor* (27: 1–23).

---

[1] *Psychology, Religion and Healing.* Section one, Chapter one, Classification I.

DEUTERONOMY

If the reader turns to 2 Kings 22 he will read the story of the finding of a book of the law by Hilkiah, the High Priest in the reign of King Josiah about 620 B.C. This book was our Deuteronomy and may be referred to in Deuteronomy 31: 9. The word in fact means the second law. Its title again contains the name of Moses because it describes, and in moving terms, his own death and disappearance from the scene which he had dominated for so long. It was a good thing that no-one knew where his body finally lay (34: 6) or they might have made it a shrine and never moved on to the Promised Land.

Scholars divide the sources of the Pentateuch into four documents called for convenience J, E, D and P. "J" is so named because the word for God is usually Jahweh or Jehovah, "E" because the word used is Elohim, "D" is Deuteronomy or the second Law and "P" is the priestly code embodied mainly in Leviticus.

We see then that Deuteronomy is largely the work of hands other than those which edited Genesis, Exodus and Leviticus and it was around 300 B.C. that the first five books of the Bible, the Pentateuch, assumed the form in which we have them today. This new strand of origin, "D", accounts for many repetitions and incidents earlier described in Genesis and Exodus including, for instance, the Ten Commandments (5: 6–21) with slight variations from the presentation of them in Exodus 20.

Josiah the King had rebuilt part of the Temple in Jerusalem, but the worship of God had deteriorated so that elements of heathen worship had complicated the simple religion Moses had taught. Even prostitution and homosexual practices had been elevated to religious ceremonies

C

(2 *Kings* 21). *It was the discovery of Deuteronomy, and the revival which followed, that halted this evil penetration and purified the religion of Israel* (2 *Kings* 23).

We have to remember that, now, armed forces were part of Israel's host though their capture of the Promised Land was by infiltration and inter-marriage as much as by victorious arms.

Deuteronomy 6: 1–9

Jesus quoted this passage when he was asked which was the greatest commandment of all (Matthew 22: 36–39, c.f. Luke 10: 27, also Leviticus 19: 18), but remember also that it was Jesus who added "*and with all thy mind*". This passage from Deuteronomy was the one worn in a phylactery "between the eyes", and enclosed in a metal tube fixed to the Jewish doorway, so that going out and coming in the Jew should be reminded of his God. The pious Jew still touches this cylinder every time he goes in and out of his house.

Deuteronomy 7: 6–9

One of the gems of the book amid a lot of grim language. The word 'holy' (verse 6) means basically something or somebody set apart for God's service. The Exodus is seen once again as the supreme evidence of this (verse 8). Such a special relationship with God carried both privilege and responsibility. The people accepted the first readily enough. But they were often slow, as we shall see, to accept the responsibility.

Deuteronomy 8: 7–18

I re-read this passage on the day men landed on the moon (July 19th, 1969) and these verses pulled me up with their relevance for today. We may summarise by saying, "Don't forget God in the hour of success".

Deuteronomy 10: 12–21

A reminder of the love of this majestic God and the corollary that we should love the stranger (10: 19).

Following this is much repetition, terrible revenge (e.g. 20: 13–14) the strict discipline by which a disobedient son, or a daughter who lost her virginity outside marriage, could be put to death (e.g. 21: 18–21; 22: 20–21), words of blessing and cursing, lists of things clean and unclean. But always there is the insistence on the one God and on the disaster which will follow any turning away from him.

Deuteronomy 18: 15

This verse calls for special notice since it was to be quoted centuries later by both Peter (Acts 3: 22) and Stephen (Acts 7: 37) as foreseeing the coming of the Messiah, which Jesus fulfilled.

Deuteronomy 26: 16–19

God makes a covenant with His people. Chapter 28 adumbrates and fills in the details of this covenant.

Deuteronomy 31: 1–8

Moses commissions Joshua to be the leader of the people. Israel, once an enslaved mob, had become a free nation with God the supreme ruler, and Joshua, Moses's chosen successor to lead the nation to the Promised Land.

The promise to Abraham that his descendants would form a nation in its own right, which at the end of Genesis seemed so far away (see p. 20), is now about to be fulfilled.

Deuteronomy 34: 1–9

The death of Moses and Joshua's assumption of leadership. The period is believed to be about the latter half of the thirteenth century B.C.

JOSHUA

By Christian standards, Joshua is a terrible book. Its events are dated around 1250 B.C. so, of course, allowance in moral judgement must be made.

But, in fact, Joshua and his military forces invaded other kingdoms with no more provocation than the German invasion of Poland in 1939 or the Russian advance into Hungary in 1956. Have we not, in this book, the historical basis of the modern "Palestinian's" argument—whether justified or not—that the land is really theirs and Israel are intruders?

Joshua 1: 1–9

The reiterated "Be strong and of a good courage" speaks to our own need today. Joshua's confidence was not to rest in his own abilities but on the fact of God's call to him (verse 9). All that was required of him was to stand firm and refuse to be deflected from his purpose.

Joshua 3: 11—4: 9

In historic times it has been known for the flooded Jordan to undercut the cliffs on both sides of a clay gorge near Adam, so that the cliffs fall into the river and block the channel completely until such time as the river overcomes the obstacle thus caused, and flows on again as before. On December 8th, 1257 the Jordan was dammed up in this way for sixteen hours, and again, following an earthquake in 1927, when a slice of one bank fell into the river near Adam and blocked the water for twenty-one hours. At Damieh—the ancient Adam—people crossed on the dry bed of the river.

We are told (3: 15) that the Jordan was in flood and that the waters "rose up upon an heap very far from the city Adam" (3: 16) so it is easy to imagine how simple it was for the Israelites to cross the river bed, since it would take hours for the waters to pile up at the obstruction and then flow down as far as the place where the Israelites crossed.

Joshua 6: 1–21

Everyone should know the story of the fall of Jericho though no-one can now say what actually happened. The story may have been a scornful way of deriding the defenders. "You've only got to blow a trumpet and the walls will fall down", though some experts have claimed that an earthquake threw down the city walls and Joshua took advantage of this natural calamity. Jericho was not a "city" in our sense. In fact it was more like a fort surrounded by a large village and bounded by the famous wall. The whole city was not as big as the Colosseum in Rome. The ruthless killing is nauseating, e.g. verse 21. Let us hope that this fiendish slaughter, so utterly senseless as well as immoral, has been exaggerated by some over-enthusiastic scribe. How could Joshua believe that such cruelty was the will of God? Partly because such things were accepted as normal in those days. Can we, in fact, with Belsen and Hiroshima to account for, claim to be so much more enlightened? But another reason was that he identified people who opposed his God with the beliefs they held. The way to destroy these beliefs, he thought, was to destroy those who held them.

Joshua 10: 6–14

No one today can believe this story of how the sun and moon stand still, the basis of which is believed to be a fragment of a ballad from the lost book of Jasper. It is dramatic poetry, not history. It may have arisen in that the Israelites were fighting up hill, so that when dusk fell in the valley, the sun was still shining on the hill-tops and the day seemed lengthened. Here we have another example of a story like that of the angels of Mons who, in the First World War, were alleged to have brought victory to the Allies. The story was really believed and passed on as fact.

It is hardly worth while to follow the story of the gradual sub-jugation and conquest of Canaan, partly through bloody battles and massacres and partly through infiltration into the lives of adjacent peoples. The deep-rooted hatreds which divide the Middle East today may well have their origin in this ancient history.

Joshua 23: 1–14
On his death-bed Joshua pays tribute to God's guidance and the fulfilment of God's promises.

Joshua 24: 15–29
Here with some pathos we read the words of the dying leader. True, he makes it seem that God will bring all manner of horrors upon the people if they turn from him (see 24: 19–21), but the book ends with the death of a leader who has accomplished his task and fulfilled his master, Moses' desires. Israel is now a nation of settled agriculturalists with armies in each tribe, not a rabble of slaves. It has achieved military might which must be respected. It is settled in a country which it believes to be God's will for it and it has, in his name overcome nearly all its enemies. These enemies were not only the settled inhabitants of Canaan—the Canaanites —but other nomad invaders from the other side of Jordan— Midianites, Ammonites, Moabites and so on, all trying to possess the "land of milk and honey", which was no longer protected—as had earlier been the case—by Egypt.

We shall watch Israel now, moving on to fuller nationhood as God's chosen people, and united only by the common worship of Jehovah. Nothing less could have saved Israel from being lost in the surrounding culture and religion of the Ammonites around them, especially with the emphasis of Canaanite religion on the fertility worship paid to Baal. We shall see how near they came, time and again, from being absorbed in this way, but were saved on each occasion by the most spiritually enlightened among them.

Similar pressures are felt by Christians today who live their lives in a society which is materialistic, and where traditional Christian morality is questioned or ignored.

JUDGES

The word "judges" did not mean what we now mean by the word. Committees of elders in each tribe heard the complaints of people, and in our sense dealt out justice. But when danger threatened, either the loss of property or the threat of war, the people would call on some notable figure, especially one of warlike ability or skill in battle, to lead them against their enemies or settle their disputes. Only thus could men like Gideon, Jepthah and Samson, round whom folklore stories gathered, become judges in Israel. Their number was made up to twelve because there were twelve tribes of Israel, not living all together but scattered through the land.

The events narrated—the bases of improbable stories—must go back to about 1250 B.C. They were written down before 620 B.C. and were included in the Canon—or authorised parts of Holy Writ—about 200 B.C.

The book was included in the Canon to fill the gap between the death of Joshua and the birth of Samuel in whose period of influence Israel had her first king, namely Saul. At the time of the Judges the Israelites were scattered about the country. The tribes had proceeded to occupy the territories allotted to them as our maps in the end of old Bibles show, but they were separated from one another by "heathen" peoples who disputed their possession and frequently fought them. We hear much of the Canaanites, the Philistines, the Amalekites and Jebusites. Often one tribe would help another against a common enemy.

The surrounding idolatry often penetrated the pure religion of Moses. Baal came in for worship. To his followers he was the god of fertility, often represented by a bull, and his shrines were on the top of the hills and Israelites frequently paid the tribute of worship to him. They were learning to become agriculturists and it was as well to keep in with the surrounding fertility cult! This was the ever-present danger we noticed at the end of the previous chapter.

They were also learning to become fighters and their frequent defeats were always ascribed to God's anger with them for deserting Him and "going after other gods". Whether a story—either written down or passed from mouth to mouth—was about a figure like Samson, or the conduct of a battle and its outcome, the writer's emphasis is always on God who rewards and punishes and whose worship alone held them together as a single nation.

With this in mind we can read some fascinating stories, remembering that they are not related in any order and are now to be looked upon as folklore stories of the Hebrew people at a very early stage of their struggle to possess the Promised Land.

Judges 5: 24-31
A picture of the savage days of old. The woman, Jael, entices Sisera, the enemy captain, into her tent in the pretence of offering him hospitality and then, as he sleeps, drives a tent peg through his temple and then decapitates him. So much for eastern hospitality!

Judges 6: 36—7: 22
Here is the magic with which they understood God to act and the method Gideon, the military "judge" or leader, used to weed out cowards from his army. But as soon as danger passed and Gideon was dead the people reverted to idolatry and made Baal their god. (See 8: 33.)

Judges 11: 1-6
The passage shows how the people, when danger threatened, turned to a strong character—though born of a harlot—to be their leader or "captain". Do not miss the sad story of Jepthah's foolish vow.

Judges 11: 30–40

Note the strength of character. It does not occur to father or daughter to break the vow made to God, however mistaken or terrible the sacrifice seems to us now.

Judges 13: 24—15: 5

Samson's riddle and revenge on the Philistines. We are well into the realm of folklore stories now. (See 15: 4.) Here is a man so strong that he could catch three hundred foxes, tie them tail to tail, put a burning torch between each pair and drive them into the standing corn of the Philistines, or that he slew a thousand of them with the jawbone of an ass (15: 15).

Judges 16

Samson and Delilah. The whole chapter is a classic. We see again the strength and importance of a vow made to God. When the vow is broken, his strength departs (16: 17ff). The pathos builds up to a climax. "He wist not that the Lord was departed from him" (16: 20). This is one of the effects of sin most to be dreaded. It can so deaden our spiritual sense as to make us unaware how far we have lost touch with God. But notice the precious gospel of another chance, "Howbeit the hair of his head began to grow again" (16: 22).

The idea that Samson could, by pulling on two pillars pull down a building whose *roof* accommodated 3,000 men and women (16: 27), beside being full inside, and that when the building fell all were killed, including himself, is plainly an exaggeration, but it is a fitting ending to a dramatic story which must, with great relish, have been passed from mouth to mouth.

The book ends significantly with the words "In those days there was no king in Israel: every man did that which was right in his own eyes" (21: 25). In the first book of Samuel we find that the need for a king became increasingly recognised.

RUTH

No one, however busy, should miss this incomparably beautiful idyll which takes us away from war and horror into an atmosphere of rustic peace.

It found its way into the canon probably because it showed the ancestry of the famous King David. Ruth, a simple girl from heathen Moab, became the great-grandmother of King David.

Perhaps it would help to outline the story. In Bethlehem of Judah, lying west of the Dead Sea, lived a man called Elimelech who was married to a woman called Naomi, whose name means "delightful" and who seems to have been as charming as her name suggests. They had two sons, Mahlon and Chilion, as delicate in health as *their* names suggest, one meant "illness" and the other, it appears, "consumption"! Strange names, unless given because, through famine and ill nourishment, they never achieved hardihood.

Anyway, famine drove the family across the Jordan, northeast to Moab. Elimelech died and the two boys, now grown up, married Moabite girls. One married Orpah and the other married Ruth. But, alas, both the men died and we have a sad picture of the widowed Naomi with her two bereaved daughters-in-law.

News comes that there is no longer a famine in Judah and the three women plan to return, but Naomi feels it is not right to drag the two Moabite women back to Judah and she advises them to return home. Orpah sadly does so, but Ruth utters the famous words in which she pledges herself to remain with her mother-in-law (1: 16–17 R.S.V.).

Ruth thus shows herself to be ready to forsake her own people, her own land and her own religion. So Naomi and Ruth return to Bethlehem, where they cause a sensation. Naomi says her name should be Mara or "bitterness", not "pleasantness".

At the time of the barley harvest Naomi remembers that she has a relative who is a wealthy farmer called Boaz, and she instructs Ruth to go and glean in his field. The law provided that the reapers should leave part of the crop for the poor (see Deuteronomy 24: 19). This was one of many ways in which the law showed compassion for the "have-not's". So gleaning was sure to be profitable, though we can sense with Keats,

> *the sad heart of Ruth, when, sick for home,*
> *She stood in tears amid the alien corn.*

However, Boaz befriends Ruth, eats with her, and tells the harvesters to leave her plenty to glean. On the advice of Naomi, Ruth offers herself to Boaz, but he is an upright man and knows of a nearer kinsman who ought to have the first privilege of raising a family by Ruth, as the law directed. However, the kinsman does not wish this and declares this before witnesses (4: 2–3), so Boaz buys a small property left by Elimelech and now possessed by Naomi and with this property Ruth is included (4: 5–10). As he says, "Also Ruth the Moabitess, the widow of Mahlon, have I bought to be my wife, to perpetuate the name of the dead ... that the name of the dead be not cut off" (4: 10 R.S.V.).

Boaz and Ruth have a son called Obed. His son was called Jesse and *his* son was David. So King David's great grandmother was not of the Jewish faith nor of royal blood, but a simple Moabitish girl.

If we turn back to Deuteronomy 7: 3 we find that marriage between the people of Israel and women of other nations was expressly forbidden. Nehemiah was to invoke this law after the return from exile in Babylon (Nehemiah 13: 24–25). Had this law been applied to Boaz to forbid his marriage to Ruth, how different their history would have been!

I SAMUEL

This book records the end of an era and the beginning of another. Samuel proves to be the last of the line of Judges and a large part of their function as leaders was thereafter carried out by Kings. We see the emergence of the monarchy with the anointing first of Saul and then of David. The history of Israel enters upon a new phase.

I Samuel 1: 1–28

Married couples have longed for children from time immemorial. In those days this was intensified by the belief that only in a son to carry on his name could a man hope for any kind of immortality. Many people, even today, feel the same. No wonder that Hannah felt that a son "asked of God" (verse 20) and given to her must be devoted to God in a special way.

I Samuel 3: 1–19

Not for the first or last time, one who receives the call of God is given a task from which he would naturally shrink (c.f. Moses and Jeremiah). All honour to Eli for urging Samuel to obey the call implicitly, though he himself would suffer as a result.

The Philistines fight Israel and even capture the sacred ark, and in the battle the two wicked sons of Eli, Hophni and Phinehas, are slain and the news is brought to Eli.

I Samuel 4: 12–22

Eli's daughter-in-law saw clearly that the 'glory' of Israel lay in God's presence with them, symbolised by the ark. Once that presence was gone, the glory had gone too. The presence of the ark, however, appears to bring disease wherever it goes among the "heathen", so finally it is sent back to Israel. Israel gradually learns that in allegiance to the true God is its strength and to depart from it is always calamitous (see I Samuel 12: 14–15, 21–25).

When the ark comes back to Israel, Samuel, now grown up, the last of the true "judges" and the first of the "prophets", sets up a stone and calls it "Ebenezer", the stone of help, for he said, "Hitherto hath the Lord helped us" (I Samuel 7: 12). Hence the meaning of the line in Robert Robinson's hymn, "Here I raise my Ebenezer". A stone was anciently believed to be capable of containing the spirit of a god.

Samuel realises that the people need a king but warns them of what this may mean (I Samuel 8: 10–18).

I Samuel 9: 1—10: 24

"God save the king" (10: 24). The words were used of Saul, the first king in the Bible, and similar words are used at our coronation ceremonies today.

Saul displeases Samuel and is rebuked by him (13: 13–14). Jonathan, Saul's son, comes into the picture as a capable military leader, but Samuel withdraws his support of Saul (15: 11 and 23) who has refused the wholesale slaughter demanded by Samuel. The latter seems to become more and more violent and intolerant, even savage.

I Samuel 16: 1–23

The choice of a new king from the sons of Jesse. David is chosen, not only to be king, but to play his harp to soothe Saul who is "troubled by an evil spirit".

I Samuel 17: 2—18: 16

The epic story of the fight with Goliath, and David's friendship with Jonathan. Saul's jealousy is aroused concerning David, but approves David's marriage to Saul's daughter, Michal (18: 28).

I Samuel 19: 1–17

Saul at first supports David, but then tries to murder him.

I Samuel 20: 11–42

The story of the arrows and the way Jonathan warns David of Saul's anger and hostility. It is a classic example of the loyalty of friend to friend.

I Samuel 21: 2–6

This is the famous incident which Christ quoted when he was challenged by the Pharisees for breaking the Sabbath, in that his disciples had plucked ears of wheat and eaten them on the Sabbath. (See Mark 2: 26, Matthew 12: 3, Luke 6: 3.) It is another example, like that of the marriage of Boaz to Ruth, where a rigid law was set aside in order to meet great need.

Several chapters here deal with the pursuit of David by the jealous Saul and his men. It may sound strange to us that one could speak with the other with a gorge separating them (see 26:13) but it should be remembered that the land was scarred by deep gorges, narrow but steep-sided, so that they could converse without the power to capture or kill. Repeatedly David had the choice of killing Saul but he spared him. It was against David's code to "stretch forth his hand against the Lord's anointed, and be guiltless" (26: 9), although David himself had been anointed by Samuel.

I Samuel 28: 3–20

Modern psychical research makes it unwise for us to dismiss the story of Saul's encounter with the witch of Endor. Samuel was dead and Saul longed for advice. It may well be that the "witch" was an unusually powerful medium who could persuade the dead to appear. Samuel says "Why hast thou disquieted me, to bring me up?" (28: 15). It is interesting that in modern psychical experience the dead are reluctant to be "brought up".[1] A similar reaction is frequently found now when a bereaved person seeks to make contact with the dead. Anyway, poor Saul gets little comfort. He is told that God is his enemy (28: 16) and that the Kingdom will pass entirely into the hand of David.

The book ends with Saul's great defeat at the hands of the Philistines, about 1050 B.C., and the attempted suicide of Saul who fell on his own sword. "So", we read, "Saul died and his three sons (including Jonathan), and his armour-bearer and all his men that day together". It is a melancholy end to Israel's first experience of kingship.

[1] See "The Christian Agnostic", pp. 274–5, L. D. Weatherhead (Hodder and Stoughton).

II SAMUEL

We have watched the children of Israel being dominated by great prophets like Moses and Samuel. We have glimpsed at the reverence given to a high priest like Eli. But the sons of both Eli and Samuel were ne'er-do-wells. We hear the people clamouring to have a king "like other nations". We note that the choice fell on Saul, though Samuel later selected David, the youngest of Jesse's sons, to be the ruler of the people.

Now we reach a point at which Saul is dead and David succeeds to the kingship. Saul's headquarters were at Shiloh, but David makes first Hebron and then Jerusalem his centre. The latter becomes referred to as the City of David. The period is about 1004–965 B.C.

II Samuel 1: 17–27

David's lament shows how deep his feelings for Jonathan were and a remarkable absence of bitterness towards Saul, who had several times sought his life.

Note that for seven years David's reign was over the "house of Judah" only, in the south around Hebron. The other tribes refused to acknowledge David and continued the strife which had long flourished between Saul and David. Now that Saul was dead they followed Saul's son and civil war prevailed. David, however, "waxed stronger and stronger" and Saul's followers grew weaker and weaker, "until", says W. M. Dodd, "with somewhat belated and fulsome flattery 'the tribes of Israel' anointed David as king

D

and his reign lasted like that of Saul, and later, like that of his own son, Solomon, for forty years." It was at this time about 1000 B.C., that David made Jerusalem, Zion, the capital city and it has remained so to this day. David's popularity was established. "Whatsoever the king did pleased all the people." (See 3: 36.) This included continual strife with the Philistines.

II Samuel 6: 2–23
We note the deep reverence for the sacred ark and the intense joy experienced in recovering it and setting it up once more in the tabernacle (see 7: 2). Michal, David's wife, rebukes his over exuberance (6: 20), but David is happy to have planted the holy symbol in Jerusalem. God is now seen to dwell at the heart of the kingdom, which by this time extended to the border of Egypt, with David as its supreme head. The reference to the ark in Revelation 11: 19 shows that it was to re-appear at the final victory of the Messiah himself.

II Samuel 7: 5–29
It is promised that David's son shall build a permanent house for the ark to dwell in. Hitherto it was housed in a tent or tabernacle. The promise (verse 16) that David's house and kingdom "shall be established for ever" shows how the belief later gained ground that the Messiah himself would be of David's line.

II Samuel 11: 2—12: 24
No one must miss the story of David's sin with Bathsheba and his shameful attempt to evade his possible paternity, when other methods had failed, by placing her rightful husband at the hottest part of a battle. Then follows his subsequent repentance, after he had listened to Nathan's searching parable of the man who had one ewe lamb taken from him.

Nathan's words, "Thou art the man", have echoed down the centuries. Psalm 51 may possibly express David's own grief and remorse at his sin. The whole incident shows that a prophet claimed the right to rebuke even a king in God's name, and that David, unlike some of his successors, accepted this claim.

Later the position was legalised (12: 24) and Solomon was born to David and Bathsheba who had become the most recent of David's many wives. Another of David's sons, by another wife, was Absalom. But he leads a revolt against David which the latter is forced to oppose.

II Samuel 18: 5—19: 4

Few passages are more moving than David's lament over Absalom even though the latter was a rebel. The love of the people for David is vividly revealed in 19: 2. Their victory turned into mourning because of the grief of their beloved king.

II Samuel 22: 1–51

A typical Davidic Psalm of gratitude from a generous-hearted man.

II Samuel 23: 12–17

A brief but moving picture of David's sense of values. He feels he cannot casually drink water which men have risked their lives to attain. So "he poured it out unto the Lord". It seems at first a poor return for their devoted service. But how much better this is than the careless use we often make of liberty and privileges won for us by the sacrifices of other men.

I KINGS

*The book opens with David on his death-bed. A dispute breaks out.
Adonijah says, "I will be king" (1: 5) and prepares accordingly,
but Zadok the priest and Nathan the prophet are convinced that
David wanted Solomon to be his successor and they persuade his
mother, Bathsheba, with themselves as witnesses, to plead Solomon's
cause. The dying king thus addresses Bathsheba: "Assuredly
Solomon, thy son, shall reign after me and he shall sit upon my
throne in my stead" (I Kings 1: 30). At the King's instruction,
Zadok and Nathan anoint Solomon. The cry rings out, "God save
King Solomon." "He shall be king in my stead," says David, "And
I have appointed him to be ruler over Israel and over Judah."
Adonijah accepts the situation and is assured of his own safety. "So
David slept with his fathers and was buried in the City of David"
(2: 10). And in about 970 B.C. Solomon comes to the throne.*

*Solomon disposes of all possible rivals to the throne, makes Zadok
the head of the priesthood, and Benaiah the Commander in Chief of
the army. Solomon proved himself astute and a good economist and
keen on commercial enterprise especially in copper mining so that
Israel prospered and its wealth became a byword, as did Solomon's
wisdom. Commercial ability has been typical of the Jews ever since
Solomon.*

I Kings 3: 5–15

Solomon asks for wisdom and the promise of it is granted to
him. Had he asked for other things (verse 11), the prayer

would not have been granted. It was true then as it is now that we are to ask in God's name only those things which are consistent with his will for us.

I Kings 3: 16–28; 4: 29–34

An example of Solomon's shrewd judgment. One of the famous stories of the Bible.

Solomon, unworried by further wars, decides to build a temple of great magnificence (6: 21–22). The parts were made to fit together before they were put in place so that there was no unseemly hammering or noise (6: 7). It took seven years to build, (6: 38) and thirteen to build his own house (7: 1) within the precincts of the Temple.

Solomon's temple must have been an exceedingly beautiful and ornate structure, with the ark, containing Moses' tables of stone, set in a holy place.

I Kings 8: 22–66

Solomon's wonderful prayer at the dedication of the Temple. It may have been cast in poetic form with the refrain "Hear thou in heaven thy dwelling place: and when thou hearest, forgive". The celebration lasted eight days and the people went home happy.

I Kings 10: 1–23

describes the visit of the Queen of Sheba from Southern Arabia. Solomon's wisdom, wealth and magnificence are dwelt on. Solomon has been described as "the copper king". He got immense wealth, largely from copper mines (called brass), and the other mineral resources (e.g. iron) of Palestine.

I Kings 11: 1–4

Clearly, Solomon deserted the religion and morals established by Moses and David. This is a sad sequel to the spirit of the prayer of dedication (8: 22–66). But it serves to show how easy it was for the nation to slip away from loyalty to the one

God and adopt the beliefs and practices of the religion which surrounded them. Yet in doing so they were abandoning the purpose for which they had been "chosen".

We read of Solomon's decease and "Rehoboam his son reigned in his stead" (11: 43). Ten tribes, however, revolt and make Jeroboam their king, of the so-called Northern Kingdom. Rehoboam—who had spoken very roughly to the people ("My father chastised you with whips but I will chastise you with scorpions", 12: 14)—reigns over only the tribes of Judah and Benjamin (12: 20). Jeroboam is king of the other tribes. The kings of Judah had their seat in Jerusalem where the Temple was, containing the ark, the symbol of God's Presence. For this reason Jerusalem came more and more to be regarded as the supreme place of worship. "You Jews say that the temple where God should be worshipped is in Jerusalem" (John 4: 20 N.E.B.).

In order to get the best value from reading the Old Testament we need not try to follow the reigns of thirty-nine kings in thirty-six short chapters, but we must be clear that, following Solomon's death the southern kingdom was known as Judah.

There is a division—never to be healed—between the South and the North. Judah and Benjamin in the South, with Jerusalem its H.Q., and Israel—the ten other tribes—in the North, with Jeroboam on the throne at Shechem. But the word "Israel" sometimes refers to Judah. Hence the confusion. The two Kingdoms existed side by side for two hundred and fifty years, sometimes fighting each other and sometimes united against a common foe.

I Kings 16: 29—17: 24

The name that emerges now is that of the prophet Elijah, and prophets hereafter are, more than kings, the people who dominate the nation and indeed, the king, which we saw happening already in the case of David and Nathan (p. 51). Elijah is a gaunt, heroic, lonely figure as brave as a lion and ready to challenge anyone, high or low, who deviated from the teaching of Moses. The time is about 870 B.C. Ahab is king over the Northern Kingdom. The notorious Jezebel is his wife who, with her husband, degrades the worship of the true God and introduces the worship of Baal. Elijah makes a prophecy of drought and then retires into the country. He can get a sparse living from the brook and the birds, and, when they fail, from a widow whose supply of flour and oil —says the story—are miraculously maintained. In response for her generosity Elijah seems to have performed a kiss of life on her dying son and saved him from death.

I Kings 18: 17–46

We shall probably never know exactly what happened as the basis of this exciting story. Elijah, the man of the country, may have foreseen a great storm gathering and lightning may have fallen at the critical moment, but without doubt the story has grown with the telling and the desire to prove the supremacy of Jehovah over Baal. The drama of the story is superb.

I Kings 19: 1–21

Jezebel's understandable fury puts Elijah's life in danger and he flees to the wilderness in deep depression and desires only that he might die (19: 4). The prophet journeys on to Mt. Horeb, the mountain where Moses had listened to God. Elijah has a supreme spiritual experience graphically described. God speaks to him in the quietness of his own heart and reminds him that seven thousand in Israel have "not bowed unto Baal" and that his successor, Elisha, will, under God, finish his good work.

I Kings 21: 1–29

Here, vividly told, is the story of Jezebel's wickedness in liquidating Naboth so that her husband could have a vineyard and how clearly we note the courage of Elijah who intervenes and, king or no king, queen or no queen, stands up for what is right and prophesies that evil will fall on Ahab's house.

I Kings 22: 1–40

The last chapter of I Kings reveals another heroic prophet

called Micaiah. Ahab, king of Israel, appeals to Jehoshaphat, king of Judah, to join him in rescuing the town of Ramoth-gilead from the clutches of the Syrians. Many "false prophets" prophesy victory in this venture but Micaiah prophesies disaster and is imprisoned; but the disaster happens and Ahab is slain. At the end of the book we read that Jehoshaphat also "slept with his fathers" (22: 50).

II KINGS

It would be well to "recap" the situation as this book opens.

Following Solomon's death the country was divided. The Kingdom of Judah—the Southern Kingdom—was governed by a direct line of royal descendants. The Northern Kingdom of Israel passed from one military leader to another and fell into corrupt and heathen practices. II Kings briefly relates the history of both up to the point where each in turn fell victim to powerful enemies from the north and was carried away into exile.

The ten-tribed kingdom of Israel, the Northern Kingdom (about 30,000 people), was taken by Assyria about 721 B.C. and passed into obscurity. The kingdom of Judah, the Southern Kingdom, was taken captive by Nebuchadnezzar, king of Babylon, about 587 B.C. This was the Babylonian captivity about which the Psalmist wept (Psalm 137). The Temple was desecrated and largely destroyed, its treasures looted and its king blinded and his sons killed.

But this book shows that the Bible is much more interested in prophets than in rulers, because it is prophets who constantly emphasise the need for loyalty to the one God and his will. We find the firm belief that the spirit of Elijah has possessed Elisha (II Kings 2: 15). We need not spend time on the story that Elisha cursed children who laughed at his bald head and caused them to be devoured by bears, (II Kings 2: 24) or the alleged causing of an iron axe-head to float (II Kings 6: 6).

It would, however, be a pity to miss the charmingly told story of the cure of Naaman, the captain in Syria who was "a mighty man in valour, but he was a leper"; though we may remember that almost any skin disease, like psoriasis and eczema, were *called* leprosy in ancient times (**II Kings 5: 1-27**). Notice how Naaman holds the ancient belief that Israel's God can be worshipped only on Israel's soil (verse 17).

Another gem in this book, II Kings, is the story of the king who, to cheer his people, wore outwardly the royal purple, but the sackcloth of mourning and sorrow next his skin (**II Kings 6: 25-30**).

Some of the stories told of Elisha seem repetitions of those told earlier of Elijah, such as dividing the waters of Jordan by striking them with a cloak, or replenishing a widow's cruise of oil, or restoring a child by the kiss of life, or the references to chariots of fire.

II Kings 9: 1-37

Jehu—whose fast driving has become a proverb—is commanded by Elisha to be King of Israel. After getting rid of Jehoram (Joram) and Ahaziah, Jehu disposes of the wicked Jezebel. Finally, the whole of King Ahab's family is massacred.

After many confused stories, Elisha later dies (II Kings 13: 20). Miraculous stories continue, however, to be told about him, such as the story of a dead man, through being made to touch the bones of Elisha, being brought back to life (II Kings 13: 21).

We read much after II Kings 18: 1 of the good reign of Hezekiah who sought to purify religion and who prepared Jerusalem against siege by erecting an aqueduct 1700 feet long which brought water secretly from a hillside. The siege of Jerusalem, when "the Assyrians came down like a wolf on the fold", failed. Perhaps some epidemic overtook the troops who lay dead in a few hours (II Kings 19: 35).

II Kings 20: 1-7

We have a moving account of King Hezekiah's recovery, after he had "turned his face to the wall", through the ministry of Isaiah and his boiled figs (verse 7).

Finally Hezekiah died and was succeeded by Manasseh and then

Amon over whose "abominations" we may pass. Josiah followed them and "did that which was right in the sight of the Lord" (II Kings 22: 1–2). We read further (23: 25), that there was no king before or after him who so "turned to the Lord with all his heart and with all his soul and with all his might according to the law of Moses".

II Kings: 1–15 (c.f. II Chronicles 34: 1–8)

Zedekiah was Josiah's successor—twice removed—whose eyes were put out and who was bound with fetters of brass and carried captive by Nebuchadnezzar into Babylon. Jerusalem meantime in 587 B.C. was captured and sacked. It looked like the end of the nationhood of the Jews. Once again God's promise to Abraham appears to be thwarted.

I & II CHRONICLES

The two books of Chronicles, together with Ezra and Nehemiah, are believed to have originally formed one book, written about 300 B.C., possibly by Ezra or some anonymous writer living in Jerusalem and connected with the Temple. By this time the fifty years of exile in Babylon were over and some of the people had returned to their home country to rebuild Jerusalem and its ruined Temple. The books of Ruth and Jonah also belong to this period.

The object of Chronicles I & II was to outline the history of the people of God in such a way as to show God's purpose being worked out in it. He had chosen them to achieve a faith in one God alone, and to maintain that faith in the face of corrupting influences in the nations around them. Every king's reign from Saul's to the Exile is treated with this in mind. Events are related to show how far the various kings kept the faith, and how those who did so prospered.

The ground covered is therefore often the same as in I and II Kings, that is, from the death of Saul to the captivities, but chiefly concerns the southern Kingdom of Judah where the royal line continued from Solomon and Rehoboam.

Here and there, however, there are gems, not to be missed.

I Chronicles 11: 15–19
This is the incident described in II Samuel 23: 12–17 (see p. 51).

I Chronicles 22: 5–13; 28: 1–10

David is not allowed to build a Temple for the Lord, but he is allowed to make preparation for it, and Solomon benefited thereby. David's words of blessing to the people are also well worth reading (I Chronicles 29: 10–28).

In the second book we can pass over the details of the splendour of Solomon's temple, but his dedication of it is worth reading again in the Chronicles version of it.

II Chronicles 6: 1–42; 7: 9–11

God promises (in II Chronicles 7: 18) that under certain conditions, "there shall not fail thee a man to be ruler in Israel" and twenty kings followed Solomon, but only a few like Asa, Jehoshaphat, Joash, Uzziah and Hezekiah "did right in the sight of the Lord", and sad events followed. Asa won his battle against the Ethiopians with the help of the Lord (II Chronicles 14: 12), but Jehoshaphat, godly to a degree, formed an alliance with Ahab the idolatrous King of Israel (II Chronicles 19: 2) and later the Temple fell into ruin; and when Jehoiakim "did that which was evil in the sight of the Lord" (II Chronicles 36: 5–7), Nebuchadnezzar, king of Babylon took him prisoner, sent him into exile, and removed much of the gold in the Temple and placed some of its holy vessels in his heathen shrine in Babylon.

Jehoiakim's son aged only eight was "king" in Jerusalem, but he too was carried away into exile. The next and last king of Judah was Zedekiah who suffered the same fate. He "transgressed very much after all the abominations of the heathen and polluted the house of the Lord" (II Chronicles 36: 14).

EZRA

To avoid confusion, it is important to distinguish between the man *Ezra, the scribe, and the* book *which bears his name. As noted on p. 60, the book was originally part of a larger one which included I and II Chronicles and Nehemiah (and may possibly have been compiled by Ezra). It describes happenings such as the first return of the exiles in 537 B.C. It also tells of the arrival in Jerusalem of Ezra himself. But over 100 years separated the two events (see the Chart on pp. 14–15).*

Similarly Nehemiah, whose book *follows the book of Ezra, himself reached Jerusalem nearly 50 years before Ezra the scribe arrived there.*

Ezra 1: 1–6

The close similarity of verses 1–3 with the last three verses of II Chronicles confirms the link we noticed (p. 60) between these books. The excitement of one's mind rises at a name in the first sentence, that of Cyrus, King of Persia.

Cyrus had now captured Babylon (539 B.C.) and what is of prime importance to remember is that the policy of Cyrus was to keep captured people in their own country with his appointed satraps, or provincial governors, over them.

Hence Cyrus not only allowed, but urged the Jews back to their own land, under the leadership of Zerubbabel, and in addition even restored the Temple vessels which the Babylonians, under Nebuchadnezzar, had plundered. These vessels were taken to Jerusalem by Sheshbazzar (1: 11) and his company was in fact the first to return from exile. The date—537 B.C.

This action of Cyrus was, attributed by all devout Jews to the providence of God, and many of the Psalms testify to their joy. "When the Lord turned again the captivity of Zion ... then was our mouth filled with laughter and our tongue with singing" (Psalm 126: 1). Isaiah, who was himself one of the exiles (see p. 92), makes God describe Cyrus as "My shepherd (who) shall perform my pleasure".

Without any doubt the period of exile, at least fifty years, deepened the faith of the Jewish people, that is, those taken only from the tribes of Judah and Benjamin with a few Levites, the priestly caste, and they subsequently showed themselves as *religious* geniuses and not a warlike nation competing with Assyria, or Babylonia or, of course, with Persia. Trial and hardship served to show the people what God's real purpose for them was. They returned from exile determined above all to establish and remain faithful to the true religion of one God alone.

Ezra 3: 8-13

Many Jews probably stayed in Babylon, even though free to return to Palestine. They had inter-married and entered into financially successful business ventures and preferred to stay in the comfort they had created, for there is no evidence that they were harshly treated in exile. They probably sent further gifts from their wealth for the rebuilding of the Temple. But the thrill of the opening of Ezra is the way in which God—as they rightly believed—had opened the way for his own chosen people to return to Jerusalem, build up its walls and restore its Temple as the centre of its life, especially its festivals, like the most important—the Passover. Above all, God has exhibited his pardon for their sins.

It may be asked whether the Jews returning from exile in Babylon met and mingled with the ten tribes of the north, but two factors are to be borne in mind; first that the returning Jews did not come back suddenly in one party, but in small parties over a long period, and secondly such northerners as remained in the land after the Assyrian conquest had mixed with and inter-married with those whom their conquerors sent as settlers.

Their descendants were the Samaritans who claimed to be the true Israel and carriers on of the Mosaic tradition and later built a rival temple on Mt. Gerizim near the modern Nablus. They came to Zerubbabel, the head of the returning southerners, and offered to help rebuild the temple (Ezra 4: 1–3), but the offer was firmly turned down on the ground that the Samaritans, through their intermarrying with the "heathen" and forsaking Jehovah were no longer true Jews or part of the "chosen people". Bitter hostility began which continued until our Lord's day when it could still be said that the "Jews had no dealings with the Samaritans" (John 4: 9). Feuds frequently persist long after the original reasons for them are forgotten. The problems of Northern Ireland in recent times are in some measure an example of this.

Ezra 4: 4–24

Incensed by this rebuff the Samaritans tried to hinder the building of the sacred walls and persuaded certain influential Persians to support them (4: 5), saying that Jerusalem was in any case a hotbed of unrest and rebellion (4: 12). This they did with such effect that the work of rebuilding came, for the time being, to an end (4: 24).

It was 520 B.C., about seventeen years after the return of the first exiles from Babylon, before any serious attempt was made to restore the Temple, and it was rather apathy from within than hostility from without that caused the failure to rebuild and restore. It took the fiery prophecies of Haggai and Zechariah to stimulate the flagging zeal of the former exiles (Ezra 5: 1–2), and little help was forthcoming from the few who had escaped the exile and remained in Jerusalem and who had intermarried with their captors. They are slightingly referred to in II Kings 25: 12, "The captain of the guard left of the poor of the land to be vinedressers and husbandmen."

Ezra 7: 1-26

Ezra's appearance at this point is believed to have taken place at a later date, about 397 B.C. He comes from Babylon to Jerusalem not as an ordinary returning exile but, accompanied by a retinue of supporters, bearing a special status and authority from Artaxerxes the king of Persia, whose letter is set out (7: 12–26). Was ever such a generous gesture made by a king to a one-time captive people?

Ezra 9: 1-15

Alas, instead of a reception by people who had remained loyal to God and kept the Jewish nation undefiled, Ezra is met with a situation that horrifies him (9: 2). He rends his garments and plucks out his hair and, taking upon himself the guilt of the people, prostrates himself before God in penitence and shame. "Our trespass is grown up into the heavens" (9: 6).

He pleads with God for forgiveness and rounds on the people for their ingratitude in the face of God's mercy in leaving them "a nail—[or literally a tent peg]—in his holy place", that is a fixed abode that had not been, and would not be, removed.

Ezra 10: 1-14, 17

Nowhere in history, one would think, has there ever been such a mission of repentance. All the people assembled before Ezra, and those who had married non-Jewish women agreed to cast their wives and children away (10: 3, 5). Anyone who would not do this within three days was himself to be "separated from the congregation" (10:8). This terrible edict—so far, we feel, from the real will of God as Jesus was to reveal him—was calculated to turn the "fierce wrath of our God" from the people (10: 14). Talk about the power of an outraged priest!

Yet we can understand his ruthlessness. Could the true religion be preserved by a people of mixed blood and therefore conflicting loyalties? Ezra was firmly convinced it could

E

not. We wonder what he made of the story of Ruth, which appeared during this period. For it told how none other than the great king David had a great grandmother who was a Moabitess!

NEHEMIAH

Nehemiah's place in the sequence of events following the first return from exile lies between the rebuilding of the Temple inspired by Haggai and Zechariah (see p. 64) and the coming of Ezra. The date is about 444 B.C.

Nehemiah 1: 1–11

Nehemiah is an attractive personality. He was "cup bearer" to the Persian king, Artaxerxes. This may mean that he was a personal attendant in various ways, or even that he tasted every dish put before the king to prove that it was not poisoned.

However, Nehemiah was a most patriotic Jew, and the ruinous state of the holy city of Jerusalem, as it was described to him, was a matter which bowed him down with distress and shame. So much so that he obtained permission from the king to visit Jerusalem with the object of rebuilding its walls.

Nehemiah 2: 1–8

The king not only gave permission but passports "to the governors beyond the river" and a pass which enabled Nehemiah to obtain, at the king's expense, timber for his rebuilding project. A wonderful gift!

Nehemiah 2: 12–16

We have a vivid picture of Nehemiah the patriot sensing hostility (2: 10), going out at night and viewing by moonlight the terrible state of the old city with its broken walls and ruined temple.

Nehemiah 2: 17–20

Nehemiah now speaks to the people of God's goodness and also that of the king in putting it into his heart to stir the people into action. This he does so successfully that, in spite of jeers and hostility, the cry arose, "let us rise up and build".

Nehemiah 4: 1–9

Chapter 3 can be omitted for it only lists those who undertake the various repairs, but chapter 4 shows the strength of the hostility against Nehemiah and his rebuilding programme. Yet the latter goes forward because—significant phrase—"the people had a mind to work" (4: 6).

Nehemiah 4: 16–18

So great, however, was the hostility centred in Sanballat, the governor of Samaria, that the builders had to be armed. One can imagine them with a sword in their belts and a trowel in their hands and with a passionate, patriotic ambition in their hearts, not to be denied, working away at this formidable task, with some of their fellow patriots, armed with bows and arrows and spears, standing behind them as they worked, and a trumpeter standing by Nehemiah himself to give warning of attack. Sanballat had called them "these feeble Jews", but in two months they had completed the repairs to the walls: an amazing achievement under such circumstances.

Nehemiah 5: 1–15

The king of Persia must have waited long for the return of his cup bearer, for Nehemiah seems to have become a kind of governor of Jerusalem; a counsellor who is consulted and who tries to right wrongs, like usury and the misappropriation of land. "Think upon me, my God, for good," he prays, "according to all I have done for this people" (5: 19). He needs the sense of divine protection, for Sanballat seeks to achieve by guile what he failed to do by arms. Nehemiah perseveres, and we read the climax on the great day when "the book of the law" is read to the people.

Nehemiah 8: 9–18
The passage ends with the festival of the booths. Although the walls were completed, many had not got their houses rebuilt and the booths celebrating the sojourn of the Israelites in the wilderness also probably provided them with some shelter until the houses could be completed within the new walls.

There follow details of the solemn ceremony at which the Mosaic Law was read to a penitent people who promised in future to stick to it (9: 38; 10: 29–39), including—and this is important, as we saw in Ezra—a promise to abstain from marriage with any woman who was not a pure Israelite. We need not read these details again. The long section ends with the words, "We will not forsake the house of our God" (10: 39).

Nehemiah 13: 1–31
In this final chapter we find Nehemiah insisting on the old Mosaic law. Was not this the foundation of the religion they were pledged to uphold? The Sabbath is not to be desecrated by carrying on business, however prosperous it might be (13: 15–19). Women who were not of Jewish blood were not to become the wives of loyal and true Jews (13: 23–27).

As the book closes we may take a look at the position. A small nation of true Jews were surrounded on every side by nations of very different characteristics and incredibly greater power and riches. Many Jews had fallen away, lured by attractive wealth and attractive women, but there was a faithful remnant even though it was more a colony of Persia than a nation in its own right.

Of this remnant we may say that they preserved the worship of the true God and amid all the opulence around them they knew that their God would work out his purpose through them and use even the great nations around them as instruments of his will. They felt that they must nurture the worship of Jehovah and hand on the traditions, ceremonies and laws of the God of Moses.

It is a monument to Nehemiah and Ezra that the paganism and immorality which surrounded them was condemned as evil, and that the pure religion of Moses with the asceticism, exclusions and intolerances should have been preserved. Israel was now a busy community settled in a tiny corner of the Persian Empire in about 350 B.C. Yet its idealism proved stronger than military might and national wealth and prestige and it became a nation into which in "the fulness of the time" God could send his Son. This crowning point of God's purpose for them was foreseen only dimly, if at all. But this was to be the fulfilment of the promise made to Abraham that "in thee shall all the families of the earth be blessed" (Genesis 12: 3).

ESTHER

The busy man can omit this book altogether, without loss. The name of God does not once occur in it and it is difficult to understand how it ever got into the Bible. What a Bantu or Hindu convert to Christianity makes of it cannot be imagined.

The book is now generally agreed to have been written between 150–100 B.C.

The story it tells is one of violence, intrigue, bloodshed and cruelty, and, although one admires Esther for intervening when her fellow-Jews were threatened with extermination, one turns with loathing from the cruel revenge she adopts in having, not only her persecutor hanged, but his ten sons and many others as well (9: 13).

The story can be told briefly. King Ahasuerus of Persia (486–465 B.C.), or Xerxes, as he was more commonly known, tires of his wife, Vashti, who refuses to obey him in this and that. His favour falls on Esther, without his knowing that she was a Jewess, and he makes her his Queen.

Mordecai, a well known Jew, is the new Queen's cousin, though this also is not generally known. He was one of the exiles from Judah, brought into captivity by the Babylonians. Mordecai hates Haman, the King's vizier and chief counsellor—we could call him the prime minister—and the hate is returned.

Haman seeks to end this feud by a wholesale massacre of the Jews, but Esther reveals that she is a Jewess and intervenes successfully to save her people.

So far so good, but then Esther demands revenge. Haman is hanged on the high gallows he had prepared for Mordecai and the Jews engage in a massacre of their enemies. "Many of the people of the land became Jews for the fear of the Jews fell upon them" (8: 17). For a story of bloody revenge the narrative would be hard to beat.

Mordecai was raised to the rank formerly held by Haman. He revelled in the revenge and ordered that a festival of "gladness and feasting" (9: 19–28) should always be kept in memory of Esther's intervention and its sequel in the massacre of all enemies of the Jews. This was the origin of the feast of Purim, a time of rejoicing and conviviality and the exchange of presents, rather like our Christmas, but with how different an origin!

JOB

Sections of this book, at least, must not be missed. It is not only one of the greatest dramas in the Bible but in the whole of the literature of the world. We do not know who wrote it or when. It really matters little to the ordinary reader. It certainly goes back to centuries B.C.

We do not know whether there ever was such a person as Job—the name could mean "the persecuted one"—or whether the writer did what Shakespeare did centuries later, took some real happening—in this case the undeserved suffering of some God-fearing man—and wove his drama round it.

The story is straightforward enough. We are presented with the picture of Job, "perfect and upright and one that feared God and eschewed evil". According to men's ideas of Divine Providence at this stage it was normal that he should therefore be favoured by God with immense wealth, with every kind of happiness and every token of success.

Then enters Satan with the sneer that Job is only a good man because goodness pays. "Doth Job fear God for nought?" So, in the drama, Satan is allowed to cause misery to fall on Job and the deprivation of all he has, including his family. Even so, Job clings to his loyalty to God. Even when he is smitten with disease and his own wife turns against him and advises him to "curse God and die", his faith is unbroken and he tells his wife not to talk like an "impious fool" (Moffatt).

Following this, Job's "comforters", enter on the stage. They have become synonyms for people who speak useless and irritating words to those in trouble. They first sit silent before Job's terrible condition,

73

but after they had finished arguing, Job "opened his mouth and cursed the day he was born" (3: 1 ff).

No argument is given which acceptably answers the problem as to why, in the hands of a God who is both power and love, a good man who loves God and serves him should be allowed to suffer so terribly.

The drama gives the only answer there is and it is an answer of faith, not of reason. It is that God is so great, above all human conceiving, that man is incapable of understanding his ways and can only believe that God must be both love and power, and that our conviction of him as both means that one day we shall understand.

Such a vision as Job had, made him feel not crushed but buoyed up by God's greatness. Such power as the heavens declared made him sure that God would vindicate his servant, and Job is penitent that he has not seen this earlier. He does not repent of sins, for he has not committed them, but of lack of faith in God's goodness and ultimate omnipotence.

When Job had his vision of God, it had the effect on him which we should experience if, for instance, we could talk with Jesus in the flesh. Queries would die on our lips and we should feel overwhelmingly certain that all was well, even though we could not understand with our intellect all that God was doing.

We cannot understand the mystery of pain and suffering, particularly of the innocent and undeserving. One thinks of a little boy whose father is a surgeon. One imagines an evil-intentioned person showing the boy his father operating, cutting the flesh of a helplessly unconscious victim. How could anyone explain? The boy has to believe from other evidence that his father is good, as well as clever and powerful, and await explanation. We shall say in the spirit of Job, "I know that Thou canst do all things and that no purpose of Thine can be restrained, and now that I have had a vision of Thee I can forget all the things said against Thee that puzzled me and repent that I ever let them make me doubt Thee."

The author of Job had to end his drama with Job restored to all his wealth and prosperity because the author had no adequate view of an after life, but only of a dim and rather meaningless Sheol or abode of the spirits of the dead. We can feel that in a life—or lives—after death we shall increasingly understand all that tortures our minds now and rejoice in an existence where, beyond this dark valley of suffering and tears, things become plain.

The book of Job is meant to teach, that what is required is not rebellion against the injustices of life, but an acceptance of what one cannot prevent or cure, in the faith that God can use it and weave it into a plan which will be acceptable and wonderful. If God is the creator of the heavens—the Bear, Orion and the Pleiades for example, he is great enough to weave man's suffering into his plan. When Job says finally, "I repent" (42 : 6) he does not mean of his sins but that his dependence, obedience, and trust in God broke down for a time.

God's ways remain an inscrutable mystery. What he allows is still veiled in darkness. But from man is asked a faith that holds on in the dark and a trust that no loss or suffering can destroy. In utter dependence and obedience, even in the dark, Job finds at last peace of mind and his rebellion against God is ended and the futility of the arguments of his friends is exposed as false as well as futile.

Job 1: 1—2: 13
Job's prosperity and wellbeing undergo drastic change. Note the sublime faith expressed in 1 : 21.

Job 3: 1–26
Here is Job at last broken down and for the moment cursing the day he was born.

Job 4: 1–9
Eliphaz, the first of the "comforters" who taunts Job with having helped others by the theory that suffering is a sign of wickedness, and success the fruit of faithfulness and now—Eliphaz tells Job—you won't take your medicine yourself. "Remember, I pray thee, whoever perished being innocent? or where were the righteous cut off?" (4: 7). This belief persisted down to the time of Jesus, but he repudiated it as *necessarily* the explanation of suffering (see John 9: 1–3).

Job 6: 1–10
Job longs for death to set him free: "Oh that it would please God to destroy me!" (6: 8–9).

Job 8: 1–22

Here enters Bildad the second "comforter". His argument is the same. Job *must* have sinned. "Behold God will not cast away a perfect man neither will he help the evil doers." (8: 20.)

Job 9: 1—10: 22

Job's answer is that in view of God's greatness, "Who will say unto Him—'What doest Thou?'" This answer of Job is splendid literature as well as logic. What a contrast this is to the attitude which can only complain, "Why should this happen to me?" He dare not argue with so mighty a Being as God, but he is full of confusion (10: 15) and cannot understand why he was born (10: 18).

Job 11: 1—12: 3

Here enters Zophar the third "comforter", but he adds nothing to the arguments of the first two. As Job fittingly says, "No doubt but ye are the people, and wisdom shall die with you. But I have understanding as well as you; I am not inferior to you" (12: 2–3). But he clings to his assertion of his own innocence and will not be shouted down by his "comforters".

Job 13: 1—15: 2; 14: 13–14

Job's mind seems to fluctuate between the thought that death is the end, and at least a query that it may not be. Here as in Chapter 19 is a glimmering of belief in an after-life. In 13: 15 Job stoutly defends his conviction that no sin of his has warranted such suffering.

Job 16

Job breaks into eloquent despair.

Job 19: 21–27

There are some legal terms here. "Vindicator" is better than "Redeemer" and means a barrister who will defend a brief, and "stand" is used in the sense we mean when we sing, "Stand up, stand up for Jesus". The Vindicator will clear Job's name and stand up for him against all his critics and enemies. Though his physical frame dies and is devoured by worms, yet from outside (apart from) his present body, in a new phase of existence with a spiritual body adapted to a new environment, he will see God to have been on his side all the time, and he will recognise the Eternal God to be his friend. There will be a double vindication. God will vindicate himself, but also the faith of the man whose faith wavered but was never lost.

It is a magnificent passage and contains a seed thought of a life that goes on after death. Job sees himself as existing after his flesh has perished.

We can omit Chapter 20. Zophar has his say with great vehemence but he says nothing new. All these friends have at heart the same philosophy from which none of them will budge: namely that illness and misfortune are signs of God's displeasure and punishment, and the "comforters" try to wring from Job a confession of some secret sin. Job, for his part, will not move from the view that he may not understand, but he will not believe what his "comforters" say for he has done nothing commensurate with what he is suffering. A verse from Chapter 32 is relevant here, "So these three men ceased to answer Job because he was righteous in his own eyes" (32: 1).

Job 23: 1–12

Job's pathetic, "Oh that I knew where I might find him!" finds an echo in all our hearts (23: 3). But he finds the answer of faith, the only answer he ever does find, "He knoweth the way that I take. When He hath tried me, I shall come forth as gold" (23: 10). Here is clearly a belief in life after death. Wickedness seems to prosper but the wicked will never finally "get away with it".

Job 28: 1–28

An eloquent statement of man's quest for wisdom and the answer can only be the same: God understands and knows (28: 23). "The fear of the Lord" (verse 28) means a healthy fear or awe which has the positive effect of making us shun evil and do God's will. Job goes on to compare the honour that was his with the scorn now poured upon him (Chapters 29 and 30) but they can be missed without loss.

Chapters 32–37 repeat the worn out argument that suffering is a moral discipline following sin. What must not be missed is God's majestic answer.

Job 38: 1—40: 2

God's argument is that he is so great, so infinitely above Job ("Where wast thou when I laid the foundations of the earth?" 38: 4) that it is presumption on Job's part to argue with Him.

Job 40: 3–5

Job admits his presumption and is penitent about his pride.

Job 42: 1–17

Job stands overwhelmed with the greatness of God and is ashamed of his own presumption in questioning. In the wonder of that vision he repents this presumption. Note especially verses 3–6 with their strong conviction that God's purpose is finally invincible.

There is today still no solution to the problem of the suffering of good people. With Christ and his cross before us we can say with greater insight than Job, "now mine eye seeth Thee", but the dearly beloved Son cried, "Why hast thou forsaken me?" and felt deserted in his greatest hour of need. No, it is no good glibly supposing that Job gets an answer to his question. We, too, can only go on clinging in the dark to the certainty that God must be both power and goodness and that one day we shall understand. In the meantime gazing at Christ, who turned thorns into a crown and a cross into a throne, we are so to react to our suffering that in the end it can be woven into his mighty purposes for our blessedness. Ultimately we shall see this to be so good that we have no question left to ask.

All this is concerned with the problem of why suffering exists. But even if we had a complete answer to this, the practical problem would still remain of how we are to react to it; what we are to do about it. The book of Job does give an answer to this.

It shows that it lies not in helpless resignation, nor even in dogged endurance. The key to Job's victory over terrible trial is his faith. Because he trusts God, he emerges undefeated. Human experience, and later, Christian experience in particular, is full of examples of this practical answer to the problem of suffering.

PSALMS

Clearly no attempt can be made in a book like this to take each psalm and attempt an exposition of it. Such expositions can be found elsewhere.

Rather, as one imagines the busy man opening his Bible at the book of Psalms, it is possible to put up a few signposts, indicating which psalms can be omitted and which should be included.

Like the early Methodists, the Jews sang their religion into the hearts of those who would listen—e.g. "Sing us one of the songs of Zion" (137: 3). While we can understand the longing for revenge over their enemies and the appeal to God to scatter and smite them, this can spoil much of the book of Psalms for the Christian, who knows that the spirit of Christ is the touchstone by which all attitudes must be assessed. The word "enemy" is said to be the commonest word in the Psalter and reflects the insecurity of the Jew surrounded by hostility on every side.

But four points lift the Psalter above all the rest of the Old Testament in any assessment of devotional value.

1. *That praise is due to God and should be joyfully and willingly ascribed to Him. See Psalm 103 and note the element of praise in scores of other psalms.*
2. *The idea dawns that God does not want the sacrifice of animals but the repentance of the human heart. See Psalm 51: 16.*
3. *That there is a life after death superior to the dim existence in Sheol which sounds so depressing. See Psalms 16: 10–11, 23: 6 and 73: 23–24.*

4. *That it is certain that in the end God will triumph over all his enemies and bring in an era of peace and plenty through His chosen people. See Psalm 29: 10–11 where the "king" is God Himself.*

We do not know who wrote the Psalms. We refer now to "Wesley's Hymnbook" without meaning that Wesley wrote all the hymns. So the "Psalms of David" are by many anonymous poets, and sometimes have had additions made to them as in the unfortunate last two verses in Psalm 51 which naturally ends at verse 17. Only 73 out of 150 psalms are ascribed to David, and even here the term translated "of David" could equally well mean "for" or "about" him.

We would be wise to remember the Psalmist's idea of a poem. Rhythm means more than rhyme, and we find a sentence followed by much the same idea in different words which together make a beautiful verbal effect, e.g.

Hear my prayer, O God;
Give ear to the words of my mouth. (Psalm 54: 2.)

This putting together of similar ideas in separate sentences is called parallelism and makes so many of the psalms pleasing to the ear even in their English form.

Some words may puzzle the reader. "Psalms" were religious songs set to accompaniments on instruments, e.g. Praise the Lord upon the harp or on an instrument of ten strings (33: 2 and 144: 9). Read Psalm 150 for a list of the whole orchestra! And note the subtle saying in Psalm 49: 4, "I will open my dark saying (N.E.B. 'riddle') upon the harp". "Selah" was an instruction to the musicians and possibly meant, "Repeat that phrase again". Asaph was David's choirmaster, and "Ethan" (89) was the chief of the guild of Temple musicians: the leader of the orchestra, we might say. The "sons of Korah" may have been a choir or company of musicians under Korah, who added doorkeeping to their musical duties (cf. 84: 10). The word "Amen" means colloquially, "For sure" or "This is certain".

The great value of the Psalter for the modern man who reads with discretion is the insight of the Psalmist into the nature of God and the spiritual needs of men. Repeatedly he brings these together in moving and beautiful language. We cannot adopt all that language, because it is spoilt by the constant craving for revenge, but much of the language can still be used to challenge, inspire and comfort the human heart. The Psalms all speak of God's adequacy to the needs of his people and they all point to a future when God shall reign and all men live in peace. To these psalms, some of them written 1000 years B.C., others as late as 200 B.C., we shall try to direct the reader.[1]

Psalm 1. Realise how eager the author is that "the way of the ungodly shall perish". This longing for vindication runs throughout the Psalter, and will not be referred to again.

Psalms 3, 4 and 5.

Psalm 8.

Psalm 13.

Psalms 15 and 16.

Psalm 19.

Psalms 22, 23, 24, 25.

Psalm 27.

Psalms 29 and 30.

Psalms 32, 33, 34.

Psalm 36 verses 5–10.

Psalm 37 verses 1–11.

Psalm 40[2] **omitting verses 14–15, but note verses 6, 7.**

Psalms 42 and 43.

Psalms 45[2]**, 46, 47 and 48.**

Psalm 51 verses 1–17.

Psalm 55 verses 1–8, 11–14, 22.

Psalms 56 and 57.

Psalm 63 verses 1–8.

Psalms 65, 66, 67.

Psalms 71, 72[2]**, 73.**

Psalm 84.

Psalm 89 verses 1–9, 14–21, 34–37, 49–52[2]**.**

Psalm 90, and, with reservations, Psalm 91.

Psalms 95, 96, 97, 98.

Psalm 100, 102[2].

Psalm 103.

Psalm 107.

Psalm 111.

Psalm 113.

Psalms 115, 116, 117, 118.

Psalms 121, 122, 123, 124, 125, 126, 127.

Psalms 130, 131.

Psalms 137 (omit verses 8 and 9), 138, 139 (omit verses 19–22).

Psalms 142, 143.

Psalms 145, 146, 147, 148.

Psalm 150.

[1] Those who feel that the Psalter should not be tampered with might well reconsider asking a modern congregation to sing Psalm 58 verse 10. Cf. also Psalm 68 verses 21–23.

[2] These Psalms are among those often referred to, by Jews or Christians or both, as Messianic. This is because they contained verses quoted by New Testament writers as fulfilled by Christ, or because they portray a future hope which could be fulfilled only by the coming or final triumph of the Messiah.

PROVERBS

The busy man may omit the greater part of this book without serious loss. My father's old Bible in the Authorised Version, which I have used frequently in writing this book, carries at the head of each page some kind of summary of the teaching on that page. In Proverbs, page after page is simply headed, "Moral virtues and their contrary vices".

The theology of the whole book is the old teaching, which Jesus contradicted (see Luke 13: 1–5), that a good man would be materially rewarded and a bad man punished. Goodness thus is a paying proposition and the sensible thing to do is to be good. Suffering means—so the argument runs—that one has turned from God's ways and followed some evil course. To strive for goodness, then, is wisdom and the opposite is folly.

The book is clearly not the work of one writer. One extols "wisdom" as the most important thing in the world (Chapter 3). Another strings together disjointed aphorisms. A third gives us the qualities that make the perfect wife (31: 10–31), while a fourth seems to have borrowed from the wisdom literature of Egypt (22: 17—24: 22).

I have heard of a man reading Shakespeare for the first time who said that the thing that surprised him most in the plays was the number of quotations! If we do read Proverbs we shall find the origin of a lot of sayings that have become part of our common speech.

I will list a few of the gems.

1: 7 The fear of the Lord is the beginning of knowledge.
1: 10 If sinners entice thee, consent thou not.
1: 17 In vain the net is spread in the sight of any bird.

3: 6	In all thy ways acknowledge him, and he shall direct thy paths.
3: 17	(Speaking of wisdom). Her ways are ways of pleasantness, and all her paths are peace.
10: 7	The memory of the just is blessed.
14: 34	Righteousness exalteth a nation.
15: 16	Better is little with the fear of the Lord than great treasure and trouble therewith.
15: 23	A word spoken in due season, how good is it!
16: 16	How much better is it to get wisdom than gold! and to get understanding rather to be chosen than silver!
16: 32	He that is slow to anger is better than the mighty; and he that ruleth his spirit than he that taketh a city.
17: 22	A merry heart doeth good like a medicine.
18: 13	He that answereth a matter before he heareth it, it is folly and shame unto him.
18: 24	There is a friend that sticketh closer than a brother.
20: 1	Wine is a mocker, strong drink is raging: and whosoever is deceived thereby is not wise.
22: 6	Train up a child in the way he should go: and when he is old, he will not depart from it.
23: 7	For as he thinketh in his heart, so is he.
24: 17	(A striking exception to the thought of the time!) Rejoice not when thine enemy falleth, and let not thine heart be glad when he stumbleth.
26: 11	As a dog returneth to his vomit, so a fool returneth to his folly.
27: 1-2	Thou knowest not what a day may bring forth. Let another man praise thee, and not thine own mouth; a stranger, and not thine own lips.
27: 6	Faithful are the wounds of a friend.
28: 1	The wicked flee when no man pursueth.
29: 18	Where there is no vision, the people perish: but he that keepeth the law, happy is he.
30: 18-19	There be three things which are too wonderful for me, yea, four which I know not: The way of an eagle in the air; the way of a serpent upon a rock;

the way of a ship in the midst of the sea; and the way of a man with a maid.

30: 25 The ants are a people not strong, yet they prepare their meat in the summer; the conies are but a feeble folk, yet make they their houses in the rocks.

ECCLESIASTES

Here is a book which may be omitted without loss. We are not surprised that when those who, in about A.D. 90–100, decided what should, or should not be included in the sacred scriptures, Ecclesiastes was all but omitted. It is almost entirely pessimistic and fatalistic and some scholars think that the more optimistic passages were added later by a more cheerful hand. No one knows who the lecturer or "preacher" was, and it is only surmise which attributes it to Solomon. The author was clearly an elderly Jew, living in or near Jerusalem, and wealthy enough to have tasted what are called the good things of life. He lived about 200 B.C. when Persian rule had given place to Greek.

Such teaching as there is, is that man may be wise and rich and prosperous only to feel at the end, "Vanity of vanity, all is vanity and a striving after wind." So he hates and despises life.

There are in the book a few passages worth remembering, e.g. the famous verses in Chapter 3 beginning, "To every thing there is a season, and a time to every purpose under heaven". For this read Chapter **3 verses 1–8.**

Other isolated passages often quoted are:

"He hath set the world—or rather, eternity—in their heart" (**3: 11** R.V. margin).

"A threefold chord is not quickly broken" (**4: 12**).

"God is in heaven and thou upon earth: therefore let thy words be few" (**5: 2**).

"The profit of the earth is for all: the king himself is served by the field" (**5: 9**).

"As the crackling of thorns under a pot, so is the laughter of the fool: this also is vanity" (**7: 6**).

"Lo, this only have I found, that God hath made man upright; but they have sought out many inventions" (**7: 29**).

"A living dog is better than a dead lion" (**9: 4**).

"Cast thy bread upon the waters: for thou shalt find it after many days" (**11: 1**).

"Remember now thy Creator in the days of thy youth" (**12: 1**).

"Or ever the silver cord be loosed, or the golden bowl be broken, or the pitcher be broken at the fountain, or the wheel broken at the cistern. Then shall the dust return to the earth as it was: and the spirit shall return unto God who gave it" (**12: 6–7**).

Finally, in a sentence which all who have studied this book will agree with, we find "Much study is a weariness to the flesh", but, "Let us hear the conclusion of the whole matter: Fear God, and keep his commandments: for this is the whole duty of man" (**12: 12–13**).

THE SONG OF SOLOMON

Here is another book which the busy man can omit altogether unless he wants to read a highly erotic love poem.

In my father's copy of the Authorised Version the heading at the top of the page is "The love of Christ and his Church", and in small print at the head of Chapter 1 I read, "The Church's Love for Christ. She confuses her deformity and prayeth to be directed to his flock. Christ directed her to the Shepherds' tents and, shewing his love for her, giveth her gracious promises. The Church and Christ congratulate one another."

It must have been possible for the ancient rabbis who determined what should be included in the Bible to see in this love poem some parable or allegory of God's love for his people. But frankly, when I read, "he shall lie all night betwixt my breasts" (1: 13) and Chapters 6 and 7, including "Thy navel is like a round goblet . . . Thy two breasts are like two roes that are twins" (7: 2–3), I know I am in the atmosphere of erotic love poetry. Even though my father's old Bible heads chapter 7, "A further description of the Church's graces", I know that the future Church's graces did not at that point dominate the mind of the poet. In fact his poem would have had no chance of being accepted into the canon unless the great name of Solomon had been tied on to it. Also the idea that it might be regarded as an allegory evidently carried some weight with its censors.

There is some beautiful language and quotable verses: "His banner over me was love" (2: 4). "Rise up my love, my fair one, and come away. For lo, the winter is past, the rain is over and gone; the flowers appear on the earth; the time of the singing of birds is come, and the voice of the turtle [dove] is heard in our land" (2: 10–12). "Many waters cannot quench love, neither can the floods drown it" (8: 7).

But, when all is said, the book cannot, without an impossible feat of mental gymnastics, be regarded as a parable. It remains a beautiful but irrelevant erotic love poem.

ISAIAH

Here is a book which we must not omit if we are to have any real grasp of the contents of the Scriptures of the Old Testament. This is the most quoted of all the prophets, not least because of its Messianic passages, i.e. those which in striking ways found their fulfilment in the life and death of Jesus.

The book is a collection of prophecies but not all by one called Isaiah. It was the habit of editors to gather together work of this kind under one famous name, just as the first five books of the Bible are called by the name of Moses, or the Psalms called by the great name of David.

We have entered now upon the books each of which—save one—is called by the name of a prophet. A prophet was not outstanding for what he foretold—like Old Moore's Almanac—so much as what he fortold—that is, told on behalf of—and what he forthtold, where in stinging sentences he said, "Thus saith the Lord".

No station in life was immune from the prophet's thrust; politicians, generals, priests, even kings were at times made to hear some unpalatable "Thus saith the Lord", in a day when, unlike our own, what God would have men do was a final authority and sanction. God counted. Life was theocentric.

The Isaiah of the earlier part of the book, 1–39, may have been a wealthy young man living in Jerusalem and functioning in the court of King Uzziah about 740–700 B.C. Isaiah (I shall use the one name though Isaiah may have been the founder of a school of prophets whose words stand under their master's name) was certain that to depart from God and to be blind to his holy will would spell disaster

*to the nation, and though he believed a remnant of the godly would be
saved, the note of doom and destruction, as well as that of promise, is
heard again and again.*

*Chapters 40–55 are by another hand, unknown, but said to have
been living in Babylon during the Exile, two centuries later, i.e.
500 odd B.C. Some scholars think that chapters 56–66 are by yet
another hand dating later than the Exile. The commentaries must be
consulted by those who wish to delve into these problems.*

Isaiah 1: 2–18

This magnificent chapter could be called, "The Great
Assize". In God's presence, meticulous sacrifices count for
little. Concern for one's fellow-men is the sign of true religion
(verses 16–17). But in the end men can rely only upon the
mercy of God (verse 18).

Isaiah 2: 1–5

A plea to the nation to turn to God.

Isaiah 6: 1–8

This is the classic account of Isaiah's dedication to God.
Uzziah had been a good king and had fathered many re-
forms. So, when he died of leprosy, Isaiah, with others,
thought it was a blow to national progress. But when the
human source of improvement passed away, the young
prophet discerned the Lord who could restore priorities and
achieve his own purpose. When the King died, Isaiah saw
the Lord and dedicated himself to God's service.

Isaiah 9: 2–7

The promise which so powerfully comes home to us through
listening to Handel's "Messiah". Peace will be established
when God alone is king, and his Messiah will be a successor
of David (verse 7).

Isaiah 11: 1–9; 12: 1–6

A typical prophecy of a glorious future, and another indication that the promised Deliverer (Messiah) would come from the house of David ("the stem of Jesse"—David's father—verse 1).

Isaiah 26: 1–9

In the famous 3rd verse the margin has, for the word "mind", "thought" or "imagination".

Much follows that is of little value for today. There are outstanding verses like 29: 13, 30: 15, 32: 2, *but some verses like* 34: 5–6 *are repellent to modern ears. With what relief therefore does one come to chapter* 35.

Isaiah 35

I find I know it by heart. It is like a poem of vision and promise. This is what the world and life can be like when all men see how good God is (verse 2) and his ways are finally vindicated (verse 4).

Isaiah 40: 1–11

We must realise that this is a different voice speaking in a vastly different situation. A situation needing indeed words of comfort, for Judah has ceased to exist, Jerusalem is in ruins as a result of the Babylonian attack of fifty years previously, and Babylon itself is on the point of being supplanted by the new power of Persia under the remarkable ruler Cyrus.

The message is addressed to the people in exile, the Jewish community in Babylon, forcibly separated in 587 B.C. by miles of desert from the rump of David's kingdom. It needed a towering faith to believe that God would even yet restore his people to their own land.

Isaiah 40: 12–31

How trivial compared with the might and majesty of God are the nations! Note the sarcasm in verses 18–20. But the

writer feels that God's true greatness is seen in his care for
the feeble.

Isaiah 41: 1–20

God will not let his people down. Again we see this dogged
faith that God's purpose for his people remains unchanged.
It rests on the evidence of history—the call to Abraham
("the man from the east", verse 2), the covenant with
Abraham and Jacob (verses 8–9) and the emergence of Israel
as a nation (verse 14).

Isaiah 42: 1–12
Isaiah 43: 1–7
Isaiah 44: 21–28

Note especially the tribute paid to Cyrus the king, "He is my
shepherd and shall perform all my pleasure" (44: 28), pagan
though he was. God does not use only his committed
followers.

*Much here can be omitted though there are some jewel sentences,
like 45: 3, 45: 15, 45: 22. Chapters 46 and 47 can be omitted and
most of 48 except verse 18. Similarly most of 49 can be omitted, but
verse 8 and verse 13 are gems. Similarly chapter 50 has verses 4 and
7 to remember, with the unrealised foresight (verse 6) of what later
happened to Jesus.*

Isaiah 51: 7–16

Note Isaiah's reiterated teaching that the greatness and
majesty of God prove that he is capable of caring for and
comforting his people. Verse 11 is word for word the same as
35: 10 which is interesting if chapters 1–39 are by a different
hand.

Isaiah 52: 7–15; 53: 1–12

This section, especially chapter 53, is among the best known
parts of Isaiah, and 53: 3 and following verses have been for-
ever immortalised by Handel's music. It is not clear who

this suffering servant is. Some believe Jeremiah is indicated. Isaiah may even have had Cyrus in mind (see Isaiah 44: 28 and 45: 1–4). The pronoun "he" may, on the other hand, have been a poetic personification of the nation which certainly has repeatedly been "despised and rejected of men". We cannot dogmatically affirm that Isaiah was consciously thinking of Jesus. This would be normally beyond his mental vision. But we can read Jesus into words which fit him so wonderfully, and I think it probable that Jesus himself, to whom the words would be familiar, thought of them as applying to himself. Some of the deepest thoughts about the suffering of Jesus come from this Old Testament writer, writing some centuries before him.

Isaiah 55

Like chapter 35 this poem is worth not only reading but committing to memory. Notice in verse 5 the theme which recurs so often—that because of Israel's faith in God, other nations would turn to them for enlightenment. 56 can be omitted, except to note that the latter part of verse 7 was quoted by Jesus when he turned out the money changers. *He* then added "but you have made it a den of thieves".

Isaiah 58

It has some obscure verses but its appeal and challenge to test religion by service to others is as up-to-date as words can be. Verses 4–14 are remarkably relevant to today.

Isaiah 60: 1–3; 61: 1–3, 10–11

Words Jesus also quoted in his first sermon at Nazareth (Luke 4: 18–19) as applying to himself. Notice that Jesus omitted the second phrase in 61: 2 ("and the day . . . God"). Other scattered verses are worthy of attention, such as 62: 5, 11–12, 63: 8–9, 66: 13.

JEREMIAH

We turn now to read the words of one whom some regard as the greatest of the prophets. Born about 650 B.C. he lived in a village called Anathoth, two and a half miles north east of Jerusalem. He was, like some modern ministers known to me, dedicated to God before he was born, and was a priest in his early twenties when we first encounter him, though, as far as we know, he never actually performed priestly functions.

His words were depressing and in modern speech we still call a depressing man a "Jeremiah" and the word "jeremiad" has passed into our language to describe a bit of gloomy prophecy or a lamentation over degeneracy.

How could one escape the feeling of gloom who pondered the situation? Jerusalem was in ruins. Jeremiah witnessed the fall of the Assyrian Empire and the rise of the Babylonian. His country lost its political independence and became a Babylonian province.

We must try to reconstruct the common reading of the situation. If Israelites were successful in battle it was because God prospered their armies, not because of good tactics or generalship. If Israel were defeated it was not through bad tactics or poor leadership, it was because God was angry with his people and used the might of Assyria or Babylon to scourge and punish them. Armies which overcame Israel were simply the instruments which God used to punish his people.

So, at a time when Israel's enemies were victorious, Jeremiah dwelt on God's anger and pleaded with the people to turn to God and thus get him on their side. He not only pleaded with the nation to return to God but, more than any other prophet, pleaded that the individual should make a personal commitment of himself to God. The words "a new covenant" (31: 31) imply an old. Jesus' words about a new covenant (Luke 22: 20) refer to the old one which Jeremiah is here pleading should be made with God by each of his worshippers.

We are to picture Jeremiah as a sad, lonely and tender-hearted young man, uncheered by wife or family, sensitive to the scorn and contempt of his own people, living an ascetic life but without ever being soured or embittered, certain that his people were in real danger and threatened with dark clouds of coming disaster, concerning which he felt he must utter his gloomy prophecies.

Jehoiakim was the king of Judah from 609–598 B.C. and the king roused the bitter opposition of the prophet, and a sermon of his, possibly delivered at the king's coronation, led to the prophet's arrest. But in response to popular demand Jeremiah was at that time released. Later Jehoiakim died during the siege of Jerusalem and his son, Jehoiachin succeeded him, but within three months surrendered to the Babylonians who sent him into exile. For prophesying the destruction of Jerusalem, Jeremiah was beaten and put in the stocks.

Jeremiah is famous for many qualities. Readers will find passages which are pure poetry. They will recognise the courage of this man. They will note his, to us, curious way of acting out his teaching— rolling in the mud, for instance, and later appearing in public with a heavy yoke round his neck, teaching by symbol that the people should submit to the yoke of the king of Babylon who, he said, was merely being used by God for a divine purpose (27: 1–22). He also wrote a letter to the exiles directing them to build houses, marry and settle down praying for God's blessing on their captors (29: 4–9).

His words are not in any recognisable sequence, and whether we owe the confusion to his secretary, Baruch, or not, we shall never know. At one time he seems to advocate fraternising with the enemy and at another—the parable of the jars, 13: 12–14—to opposing them. It was for advocating giving in to the Babylonians that his enemies threw him into the muddy cistern.

It is thought that he was carried to Egypt by some pilgrims and finally stoned to death by exasperated fellow countrymen.

We shall pick out from his prophecies those words which seem relevant to our modern day life. Without doubt this man, though doleful and gloomy, believed in a loving God whom he described as the *husband of Israel* (2: 2) *and the father of the nation* (3: 19), *and as one who, in Dr. G. Adam Smith's lovely translation, was "loyal in love". "I have loved you", Jeremiah makes God say, "with an everlasting love"* (31: 3).

Under all his gloom is a shining faith that God will restore and continue to bless his people who will return to him and enter a period under good government, in their own land. In this his robust faith matches that of Isaiah (chapters 40 *and* 41).*

Jeremiah 1: 4-12
In spite of his early dedication to the priesthood (see p. 96 and 1: 5), Jeremiah was reluctant, as Moses, Aaron and others had been, to undertake his God-given task. In the dark days of the nation Jeremiah sees the hopeful sign of an almond tree, the harbinger of Spring. The apparent "non sequitur" of God's reply (verse 12) is resolved when we learn that in Hebrew there is a pun. "Almond tree" in Hebrew is *shaked*: "I will hasten" (R.V. "watch") is *shoked*.

Jeremiah 1: 13-17
Jeremiah thought he foresaw a threat—a seething pot—in the shape of Scythian nomads from the Caucasian steppes sweeping down from the north. This threat did not materialise and Jeremiah felt God had let him down and he was discredited.

Jeremiah 2: 4-13
Jeremiah pleads with the people to return to God and reminds them of all God had done for them.

Jeremiah 3: 12-19
Another plea in which Jeremiah sees God as the bridegroom of Israel. See verse 14 "I am married unto you". We remember that Jesus called himself the Bridegroom. In verse 19 God is called "father". It is as though Jeremiah cannot find a simile which makes God's relationship with his people close enough.

Jeremiah 7: 1–11

Jeremiah pleads for sincerity in worship among the people. There is a close parallel here with Isaiah 58, since both prophets insist that true worship must issue in concern for others in need. Verse 11 makes us feel that Jesus was familiar with this book of Jeremiah (see Mark 11: 17).

Jeremiah 9: 23–24

After much that has little meaning for today, suddenly two verses ring a response from our hearts.

Jeremiah 10: 1–16

A brilliant and sarcastic comment on the worship of idols. He would surely be just as devasting on the subject of our modern idols of money, status, possessions and power. See also 11: 12–14.

Jeremiah 13: 1–9

The parable of the girdle must have been an adventure in the mind of Jeremiah, for the Euphrates was an impossible distance from Anathoth and has, at its nearest point, no rocky banks as I can testify from my own journeys in this area. It is just another parable of the ruin of the nation if it would not turn to God.

Jeremiah 18: 1–6

The parable of the potter which is famous. The words in verse 4, "He made it again another vessel" form the only oasis of comfort in a desert of gloomy prophecy. Like the potter, God never relents in his good purpose, even when dealing with the freewill of man—which is a good deal less malleable than potter's clay!

If one reads chapter 19 one is not surprised in the following chapter that Jeremiah was put in the stocks (20: 2).

Jeremiah 23: 5–6

A prophecy which looks forward to the Messiah.

Jeremiah 24: 1–10

Verses 8–10 contain the awful vindictiveness that makes the modern reader unwilling to read more, though after Chapter 26 the book contains less vindictive cursing. Certainly the prophesies are courageous if unpalatable. Jeremiah comes near being put to death for advising the people to put their necks under the yoke of Nebuchadnezzar, king of Babylon (27), though he adds (28: 3) that in two years all will be restored. A real yoke, as we have seen, was worn by Jeremiah as a symbol and was subsequently broken and removed by Hananiah (28: 10).

Jeremiah 28: 1–17

Jeremiah, however, later prophesies yokes of iron instead of wood and says that Hananiah will die within the year, which he does.

Jeremiah 31: 31–34

Jeremiah is imprisoned by Zedekiah for his gloomy prophecy but he buys a field at Anathoth, his native village, as a kind of prophecy in action that God will restore the fortunes of Israel (32: 1–15)—a striking evidence of his faith in the eventual fulfilment of God's purposes.

Jeremiah 35: 1–7

The origin of the Rechabites whose Order exists to this day, though they do not "dwell in tents"!

When Jeremiah finds himself unable, through imprisonment, to prophesy, he commits his messages to his faithful secretary, Baruch, who proclaims them. But they are still gloomy prophesies of the way God will use the rod of Babylon to chastise his people.

Jeremiah 36: 1–32

Jehoiakim, King of Judah, hears this prophesy and slashes it with his knife and consigns the portions to the fire, but Jeremiah has a "carbon copy" or rather, another edition (verse 28) containing a curse on Jehoiakim (verses 30–32). For this Jeremiah was flogged and imprisoned in a miry pit where he was left to die (38: 6).

Jeremiah 38: 7–16

An Ethiopian servant secured his being taken from the pit. This was a brave action, taken at great risk to himself. It saves the prophet's life, but he is still a prisoner, though he exacts a promise from Zedekiah that he will not be put to death whatever he prophesies. He was still with Zedekiah when Jerusalem was taken by the Babylonians. He was treated well but tradition says he was carried off to Egypt and stoned to death. Poor Zedekiah was bound in chains, his sons killed before his eyes and then his eyes were put out (52: 10) and he was imprisoned "till the day of his death".

The last days of Jeremiah were apparently spent in one prophecy after another. He was a brave and lonely soul whom some think to have been the one referred to in Isaiah 53, "He is despised and rejected of men". More than any other prophet, Jeremiah realises the weakness of formal religion. There must be, as the inspiration of all worship, a personal commitment on the part of the believer.

LAMENTATIONS

This is a book which could be omitted entirely. It consists of five dirges. The subject is the fall of Jerusalem in 586 B.C. They are acrostically arranged and certainly not written by Jeremiah. Indeed— the scholars tell us—not all are written by the same author, though the acrostic form suggests one final editor.

One verse sticks in the mind (1: 12) because it has been set to music in Stainer's *Crucifixion*: "Is it nothing to you all ye that pass by? Behold and see if there be any sorrow like unto my sorrow which is done unto me wherewith the Lord hath afflicted me in the day of his fierce anger." These words are applied in this cantata and elsewhere to the sufferings of Christ, but no sentiment could be further from his mind and attitude.

In Luke 23: 27 we read of certain women who "bewailed and lamented him". But he rejected their lamentations. "Daughters of Jerusalem," he is reported as saying, "Weep not for me, but weep for yourselves, and for your children." Jeremiah may have used such words as in 1: 12, but Jesus could not have used them or spoken of the "fierce anger" of God, his loving Father. God was "in Christ reconciling the world unto himself" (2 Corinthians 5: 19).

Prophets persistently prophesied what would happen to cities and nations that turned away from God, and the importance of returning to God runs through the five lamentations. We can sympathise with one who had seen his beloved Jerusalem made desolate, and his country overrun by its conquerors. Six centuries later Jesus wept over that same city (Matthew 23: 37), and in his bitter cry, "O Jerusalem, Jerusalem . . ." voiced a similar warning.

The lamentations are depressing and often tedious reading, but we are not left without one ray of light in all the darkness. In Chapter 3: 22–3 we read, "His compassions fail not. They are new every morning", and again, "The Lord will not cast off for ever" (3: 31). We are left with an enthroned God (5: 19), "Thou, O Lord, remainest for ever; thy throne from generation to generation".

EZEKIEL

This will not prove an attractive book for the busy man of today. We lose interest in the prophet's ecstatic utterances and the minute directions for rebuilding the Temple.

As for the prophet himself, we are to think of a young, married priest in exile in Babylon, whither, with hundreds of other captives of his race, he had been transported from the Holy Land after Nebuchadnezzar's victory in about 597 B.C. (II Kings 24: 10–16).

He was an abnormal type of man whom today we should probably label "psychic". He went into trances and saw visions and behaved in odd ways (see chapters 4 and 8) to get over his message to the people.

Life in Babylon seems at first to have been harsh, but comparatively soon captives were evidently allowed and encouraged to build their own houses and enter trade.

When Ezekiel was taken captive, Jerusalem was still intact, but after he had been in Babylon some years it fell (586 B.C.) just as Jeremiah had prophesied.

Ezekiel, like other prophets, always interpreted a set-back in Israel's fortunes as punishment by God for Israel's behaviour, in turning from Jehovah to the false gods of their captors. Yet God remained on the throne and the victories of his enemies were only his way of punishing his people whom one day he would restore.

It was this brave sounding of the note of final restoration that held Israel together and guarded against the real danger of her history coming to an end in absorption. Certainly, Israel was culturally, morally and especially spiritually, far in advance of her captors and even when the Holy City was captured and the Temple services in Jerusalem discontinued, the spirit of their religion was kept alive by words like those of Ezekiel and by the emphasis which was now placed on rites like circumcision, the laws of Moses and so on. The Temple might be temporarily lost to the nation but not the rites and ceremonies which needed no Temple.

Scholars tell us that at this time dietary tabus became an obsession, and it is clear that any ceremony that could be celebrated in captivity received a new importance now that the external ceremonies could no longer be carried out. The Temple might be lost for the time, but not the principles which brought it into being—and one day it was promised the Temple would be rebuilt and the city restored. Devotion, which could not be expressed in spectacular celebration, was all the more emphasised in the ritual, the dietary laws, circumcision, Sabbath keeping, and so on, which no disaster could hinder.

The book proclaims the majesty and glory of a God who is still the God of his chosen people. They were not forgotten and would one day be redeemed in great power and glory.

Ezekiel 1: 28—2: 10
Whether the people "hear" or "forbear" (verses 5, 7), they must receive the message and be given the chance to obey.

Ezekiel 11: 17–20
It needed a towering faith to proclaim this message in captivity, with the nation's history apparently at an end.

Ezekiel 33: 30–33
Encouragement for the prophet in dark days.

Ezekiel 34: 25–31
A sign of the slowly dawning hope of a Deliverer to come, from the lineage of David.

Ezekiel 36: 21–28
Cf. verse 22 and Psalm 23: 3.

Ezekiel 37: 1–28

The famous parable of the dry bones. Only God can give life, and without it man is helpless.

The remainder of the book is to us wearisome and unprofitable and it is with relief that one comes to the closing sentence (48: 35), "the name of the city . . . shall be, The Lord is there".

DANIEL

It is generally agreed that this book was written during the rule of Antiochus Epiphanes (175–163 B.C.), the Greek ruler of the Jews who fiercely persecuted the Jewish religion. Its first purpose is to show past heroes faced with a similar situation and how their unswerving trust in God enabled them to resist the attacks on their faith.

We notice in the Old Testament that sometimes Jewish men and women, even while they are in captivity as slaves, rise, by reason of their wisdom and ability, to positions of power and influence. Joseph is an outstanding example. He rose to a position only second to Pharaoh. Nehemiah is another case. He was the king's cup bearer.

In a similar way Daniel, the Hebrew prophet, through his ability to interpret dreams, became the "third ruler in the kingdom" (5: 29). There is a hint in 1: 3 that he had royal blood in his veins.

Like all great men who have succeeded where others have failed, he was the victim of jealousy. His enemies succeeded in poisoning the mind of the king against him.

Daniel 3: 1–30

Here we learn that three of Daniel's friends and lieutenants, Shadrach, Meshach and Abed-nego, were cast into a "burning, fiery furnace".

Don't miss the sublime faith, which is as relevant today as ever, where the heroic three say, "the God whom we serve is able to deliver us from the burning, fiery furnace, . . . *but if not* . . . we will not serve thy gods nor worship the golden image which thou hast set up." Many wonder why a loving and omnipotent God allows good men and women to suffer as they do. How sublime the faith that says, "He *could* deliver us, but if for reasons we cannot understand, he does not, still we will not lose our faith in his ultimate goodness and unbreakable love." It is a great story which lost nothing as it was handed down from one generation to another.

Daniel 5: 1–31

Belshazzar, Nebuchadnezzar's son, becomes king and held a great feast, the story of which is told.

Here is the origin of the oft quoted phrase, "the writing on the wall". It was written in Aramic not Hebrew. At the Queen's suggestion, Daniel is brought in to interpret the writing for the terrified king. "Thou art weighed in the balances and found wanting." In that same night Belshazzar the king is slain (5: 30) and Darius reigned in his stead.

But once again jealousy was aroused. Daniel would not worship pagan gods and is cast into a den of lions.

Daniel 6: 1–24

The king, after a disturbed night, finds with immense relief that Daniel is safe and well and believes that God shut the mouths of the lions. "So Daniel prospered in the reign of Darius, and in the reign of Cyrus the Persian" (6: 28).

Daniel 7: 13–14

This may possibly be the source of "the Son of man" as Jesus used the phrase. Daniel's visions may well confuse and bewilder us and can be omitted, though his cry of penitence —9: 18–19—is moving, as is his restoration in Chapter 10: 19. It is interesting that in Chapter 10 Daniel speaks in the first person. In order to see the purpose of the prophecies which follow we have to recall that the book of Daniel is believed to have been written in the time of Antiochus Epiphanes, the Greek ruler (175–163 B.C.). See above, p. 107. By this time the return from the Exile was nearly four hundred years past and yet Israel's fortunes were still at a low ebb.

So Daniel is made to prophesy the course of history which had in fact followed (11: 1–39), and to look forward to the near future in confidence. In spite of so many setbacks, God's purposes for his people would be fulfilled. He prophesies the course of the Persian Empire, then its fall and the rise of the Grecian (11:3), the fall of the Grecian and the rise of the Roman (11:40 ff.), and hints at the fall of the Roman (11:45) and the rise of a world wide Kingdom of God (12: 1–3). This would bring us to the time of Christ when Rome was a world power. The visions aim at showing that God is the supreme ruler of history and that kingdoms rise and fall according to his will.

We leave Daniel, a "man greatly beloved" (10: 19), with his final prophecy of resurrection (12: 2–3). "They that be wise shall shine as the brightness of the firmament and they that turn many to righteousness as the stars for ever and ever."

HOSEA

Hosea is one of the important group of eighth century prophets (which included Amos and Micah), and is therefore some hundreds of years earlier than the book of Daniel.

Hosea is a lovable character who sustained a disastrous marriage. He seems to have had three children who are given the most sinister names. The first child was legitimate and then his wife played the harlot and was unfaithful to him. He threatens reprisals (2: 2 ff.), but his love for her is not eradicated and he reflects that Israel in the sight of God stands in much the same relationship to God as his wife does to him. Israel has followed other gods, "played the harlot" and offended against the Lord, and yet God continues to love her as a good husband his erring wife.

There is something very important here. We are not listening to a gloomy recital of the doom which will fall upon a wicked people. There is a new note of tenderness, compassion and forgiveness and the restoration of a broken relationship.

Further, there emerges more fully than ever before the idea of Israel as the bride of God (cf. 2: 19). "I will betroth thee unto me for ever; yea I will betroth thee unto me in righteousness and in judgment and in loving kindness and in mercies. I will even betroth thee unto me in faithfulness and thou shalt know the Lord." Without doubt Jesus read these words and pondered them.

This idea of God as the husband of an erring wife, Israel, came to be established in Jewish thought, and the Church has never taken the idea up with the importance it deserves. The Passover feast opened with the declaration, "Behold, the Bridegroom cometh," and Jesus several times referred to himself as the Bridegroom, and to his men as "the children of the bridechamber" (Matthew 9: 15, Mark 2: 19, Luke 5: 24; and cf. Matthew 25: 1, where the ten virgins hope to meet the bridegroom).

In my book, *A Plain Man Looks at the Cross*, I have tried to show that the death of Jesus is best understood as his utter self-giving in love for his bride, the Church. We still tell the bride and bridegroom at their marriage that it "signifies the mystical union that is between Christ and his Church" and Paul tells the Ephesians (5: 25), "Husbands love your wives as Christ loved the Church and gave himself up for her" (R.S.V.).

"On Calvary," wrote Dr. Maltby, "Christ betrothed himself for ever to the human race, for better for worse, for richer for poorer, in sickness and in health",[1] and the Book of Revelation stresses the idea of the Church as the bride and Christ as the bridegroom. As we sing:

> *From heaven He came and sought her*
> *To be His holy bride;*
> *With His own blood He bought her,*
> *And for her life He died.*

I must not stay on this fascinating theme save to point out that the idea of God as husband and Israel as erring wife goes back to Hosea in the eighth century B.C. In Hosea 2: 16 we read, "Thou shalt call me ISHI" (= husband) and "shalt call me no more BAALI" (= Lord).

With all this in mind read: **Hosea 2: 12–23; 6: 1–6; and especially 14: 1–9,**

Out of Hosea's domestic unhappiness emerged one of the most important and comforting ideas about God.

[1] "The Meaning of the Cross" p. 10 (Epworth).

JOEL

The main interest of the book of Joel for the Christian is that it is his prophecy which is read to us every Whitsunday, and which Peter declared came true on the first Whitsunday. "And it shall come to pass afterward, that I will pour out my spirit upon all flesh . . . ." Read Joel 2: 28–32, and Acts 2: 17–21.

Joel was probably a young, patriotic priest. His prophecy was written, the scholars think, as late as 444 B.C. Such a date separates it from Micah, Amos and Isaiah by over 200 years.

Joel may have heard the story of a cosmic catastrophe which is said to have happened just before Israel left Egypt when the orbit of the earth passed through the tail of a large comet (see p. 22). The dust of the latter blotted out for a time the light of the sun ("the sun shall be turned into darkness", 2: 31) and even when the earth was almost through the comet's tail, the moon looked as red as blood ("the moon into blood").

So when Joel prophesies further outpourings of God's Spirit on men he thinks it is certain to be accompanied by strange phenomena in sun, moon and earth.

Noting then that for Joel, as for all the prophets, a natural calamity was a Divine message, the terrible invasion of locusts which Joel witnessed was for him, as for all the devout of his day, a terrible "sign" of God's displeasure.

Joel 1: 2–13

The words "palmerworm", "cankerworm" and "caterpillar" all refer to the terrible locust invasion, and they may represent locusts at different stages of growth, or be a poetic repetition of the various words for the insect, in order to get the effect of wave after wave of an invading army to which the locust-invasion is likened.

I am not surprised that Joel refers to an invading army with strong teeth, the locust has sharp, saw-like teeth. One writer speaks of an awful feeling of helplessness as one watches the cloud of insects flying low and actually blotting out the light of the sun. He says it was a cloud more than a mile broad and dense enough to make it not only dark but cold. The noise, he says, was like rattling hail or the crackling of a bush on fire. Each insect is almost harmless by itself, but in such swarms they devour everything in their path, even trees are left white and stripped of their bark. After such denudation the dried wood and withered branches make a forest fire likely. Chapter 2 is a vivid description of the calamity. Chapter 3 tells of the forest fire.

We can imagine what a terrible calamity this can be in an agricultural community. The food of animals having been destroyed, the animals die, and—a thing that distressed Joel the priest deeply—the sacrifices of the Temple which had been offered without cessation for centuries came to an end because there were no animals left to offer on the altar.

What we should regard as a natural calamity Joel, the child of his day, regarded as sent by God to punish the people of Israel for their carelessness and wickedness.

Today we cannot subscribe to that view, to that way of looking at things. Today an aeroplane scattering DDT could destroy an army of locusts in a few minutes. I was amazed when I visited Ceylon in 1951 to find that my hostess had arranged a party on the lawn in the moonlight after dinner so that I could meet the missionaries and their wives. In my time in the East, we should have been almost devoured by mosquitoes. Certainly no party could have been held out of doors in the evening. But I was told that spraying DDT from low flying planes had ended all that.

Now it is very hard to suppose that an invasion of insects is a Divine punishment for sin if it can be warded off by

DDT. Can man then snatch the whip of discipline from God's hand?

It is sounder not to link natural calamities with Divine punishments, but I cannot help wishing that we had not swung quite so far in the opposite direction. When there was a total eclipse of the sun people gathered and sang "Abide with me". A great natural event called forth thoughts of God. An earthquake or a cyclone or a flood will make people think of God and the strange meaning of life, but perhaps we have drifted too far from the theocentric mind of Joel. Certainly Jesus had the mind that flies to God along every path which nature opens up.

I think part at least of Joel's message to the busy man might well be that, while we do not equate the storm with God's anger, or the natural calamity with God's wrath, we should not become insensitive to God's desire to speak to us in all the events that happen to us, whether we call them good or evil. The heavens still declare his handiwork, the sparrows his care, and the lilies his beauty; and even the storm, the earthquake and the flood make us ponder on the forces at the disposal of him with Whom we have to do.

Joel's main message, however, is that of what he calls, "The Day of the Lord". See Joel 1: 15, 2: 1,11 and 31, 3: 14 and 18. All through the Old Testament the note is sounded of hope, and indeed, certainty, that God *will* act. His promises *will* be fulfilled. Man's dreams *will* come true. Read Isaiah 35 as a sample. "The wilderness and the solitary places *shall* be glad, and the desert *shall* rejoice and blossom as the rose." A day will come, say all the prophets, when God will break through and vindicate the righteous.

This hope buoyed men up for a thousand years and blossomed in the promise of the Messiah.

For the modern Christian several lessons are to be learned from Joel's prophecy and its consummation at Pentecost.

1. We know that whatever appearances may say, God is in charge of his world. His values endure and will be vindicated.

2. Whether we believe in a visible Second Coming or not, we must believe in a worthy climax to the human story. We

just cannot imagine the end of history. We cannot guess at a day of the Lord so final that no other day can follow it. We cannot imagine time stopping, neither can we imagine that time goes on for ever. We use words like "the end of the world", but unless indeed the earth is burnt up in some cataclysm or life on earth is in some way ended we cannot fill out the phrase the "end of the world" very usefully.

3. Most importantly, God's emergence into life depends to some extent on human preparedness. This I think was not clear to Joel.

Then and only then can there dawn a Day of the Lord, such as Joel foresaw, when the whole world, including perhaps the strange world we call Nature, with its seeming contradictions, can reflect in unbroken perfection the pattern and purpose of God.

Joel 2: 25–32;
Joel 3: 13–20

AMOS

I have often wished that I had time and ability to write and produce a play. Drama is such a powerful purveyor of ideas. The story of Amos would make a grand theme. The period is about 750 B.C. The scene is Bethel. The occasion is a great feast day to be attended by the king himself, Jeroboam II. It is held on the Sabbath, for one of the current evils was the partial desecration of that sacred day. A service will be held in the Temple and the High Priest himself, in wonderful robes, will officiate. His name is Amaziah. There is the sound of merriment and festivity in the air. Never were the fortunes of Israel so prosperous. The streets are crowded with holidaymakers dressed gaily in their brightest clothes. Jeroboam, the king, comes slowly down the crowded street in his glittering chariot. Altogether it is a colourful and exciting scene.

Standing by the pillar of a balcony is a rough, uncouth figure, wearing the clothes of a peasant. He seems to be a shepherd and carries the typical staff with the crook. A rough sheepskin is thrown over his shoulder. He has deep, piercing eyes made keen by life in the desert where eyesight is sharpened; where failure to see quickly that movement half behind a rock, that slither beneath a desert tamarisk bush may mean the loss of a sheep to a lion, a bear or a snake.

It is Amos, no priest but a layman, uneducated but, though country-born and bred, a man with insight and with passion for the welfare of his land.

In imagination we follow this man as he beckons us. Behind the feasting and the fun, he moves down streets littered with filth and garbage. We see where the poor live in foul mud huts. We note the poverty and the hunger. We note the signs of slavery of the worst kind. We listen to one man who has sold his daughter into slavery that he may keep alive the remainder of his starving family. We listen to a woman whose husband is in prison because he could not afford to bribe the judge more highly than his opponent. Even the priests, though they keep the services going, are living immoral lives . . . The times, superficially so prosperous, are, in fact, ripe for a terrible nemesis.

Amos wends his way back to the gay and laughing crowd, and there, in the great open space in front of the Temple, he speaks. The whole nation is in peril, he tells them. The rich have become cruel and heartless. The Temple stands only for an ornate ritual. Justice is no longer done in the courts. Fair trading has long given place to cheating. Immorality eats at the heart of the nation, and God will not be much longer mocked. God Himself, Amos says, takes no delight in their solemn assemblies.

Amaziah, the priest, is not going to stand for that—and on a festal day, and just outside the Temple. He thinks to silence Amos. Who is he to prophesy? He is not even a priest! Let him get back to Tekoa, his home, where he belongs. Who is he, a crude herdsman, to criticise the Temple services? God is satisfied so long as the correct ritual is carried out. Does Amos think that a great Being like the God of Israel cares about trifles like a weighted scale? Or a tip slipped to a judge, or a young girl sold to an old Jew for half a shekel?

But a prophet who is really a prophet is not so easily silenced. Amos is compelled to go home, to the village on the bleak, limestone ridge, twelve miles from Jerusalem, where he dressed (or crushed) sycomores (a species of fig, not the sycamore trees we know) and where he tended the special breed of mountain sheep that flourished there. Amos gets hold of a young scribe and dictates the book we have here, one which set going the great prophetic movement of the eighth century B.C.

Amos 3: 1–8
The people were aware of their *privilege* in being God's chosen people. Amos confronts them with the *responsibility* which it no less carries (verses 1, 2). When we read his thunderings against luxury which made rich men cruel to

the poor, against dishonest trading, against bribery which made justice a farce, against ritual which made religion meaningless, against the changing forms of evil that harass men, dare we shut the book, unable to find any message relevant to our day?

I shall pick up three messages for today from the book of Amos. The first two are not so important as the third, and I will pass over them quickly.

Amos 7: 10-15

1. We must always make a place in religion for the layman to whom God has spoken. Amos was proud of it. "No prophet I," he shouts, "nor prophet's son, but a herdsman and dresser of sycomores, but God took me from the flock".

I applaud the system of ordaining elders in the Presbyterian Church, and of using them in the work of pastoral visitation. I can find no rule in Congregationalism which would prevent a layman from preaching and from administering the sacrament. In Methodism, under certain conditions, a layman may administer the sacrament, and so can a Deaconess. In Methodism there is a large body of trained lay-preachers, and on any one Sunday they conduct five out of every seven services over the country as a whole. I would like to see laymen taking a greater part in the pastoral work of a church. I believe myself in what John Wesley called "the priesthood of all believers". It is convenient to train some men in theology and psychology and in the study of the scriptures, and to set them aside to give all their time to the ministry. But every church member should feel to some extent the responsibility a minister feels. Dean Inge said, "The Christian Church was founded by laymen for laymen". That being true, I would rather say, all are priests. Because of this, I would gladly take the Holy Communion from the hands of a charwoman.

The story of Amos reminds us how an untrained layman brought a healthy, searching wind of reality into a priest-bound, stuffy situation.

2. Secondly, Amos's attack on the ritual of the Temple. Any order of service is a ritual and is capable of falling into the dangers of all ritual. The ritual of unbeautiful dullness can separate us from God just as much as over-elaborated forms of worship. We need to listen to that warning about the dangers of development of ritual which Amos utters.

For ritual can replace reality and the burning words of Amos are not out of date.

Amos 6: 1–8

3. The third message from Amos that I want to apply to our-selves is that of the changing forms which evil takes. Israel was free from her enemies for the moment. She did not realise that in other more insidious ways, more dangerous ways, she was being attacked.

We are told by Gibbon that Rome fell, not through her exterior enemies, but through her interior vices. Are we in any different case? We have been delivered from our out-ward enemies, but complacency should be shattered by some things that are eating away the health of the nation. I would list:

(a) *Our reluctant service.* Not only shall we be unable to keep our place among other nations, but we shall lose our own self-respect unless religious revival changes our attitude to work. We used to be so proud of giving an hour's best service for an hour's pay. Now, by and large, we ask, "How can I get more and do less?" It is not the exception, but the rule to find people who come late, linger over "elevenses" and tea-time, and are dressed for home ten minutes at least before the hour they are supposed to cease work. It is cheating, of course, though the word would be resented.

(b) *The gambling fever.* In some families, I am told, the major pre-occupation of the family each week is the filling up of football pools.

(c) *The present instability of marriage.* In one recent year, divorces averaged a thousand a week. Think what that spells in terms of insecurity in the lives of little children. Physically they are catered for, but emotionally they are shattered.

(d) *The slipping down of our ideals in regard to sex.* Homosexuality rages and it is forgotten that the evil of this vice is that its boy or girl victim frequently grows up to be a homosexual. Promiscuity and sex outside marriage are tolerated in this too permissive society.

(e) *The apathy of satisfied ignorance.* Many never read a book or anything beyond the cheap newspaper. How eloquently we find Amos still speaking to us from the eighth century B.C.!

(f) *The insidious effect of drink and drugs* which can so easily enslave our young people who, for the most part, have fine ideals of service to the community and a sensitiveness to injustice and slums.

For our own secret sins Amos has a vivid reminder of the way temptation alters its form so as to make us fall. Listen to this (5: 19): The darkness of evil, he says, is "as if a man did flee from a lion and a bear met him, or went into the house and leaned his hand upon the wall and a serpent bit him". Was it a bit of autobiography? In the desert a man hears the soft pad of a lion behind him. He stops and the lion stops. Then the man takes to his heels, leaps across some stream, remembering that the great cats hesitate before they plunge into water, and scrambles up among the rocks on the other side, only to find that from behind one of them out steps a bear. The man dodges among the rocks, the bear lumbering after him, and, making a detour, the man spies the hut which is his home. Breathless and panting, he reaches its seeming safe refuge, slams the door behind him, puts out his hand to lean against the wall for support, and a snake from the ledge above him drives its fangs into his hand. What a picture of temptation, of the insidious way in which evil changes its forms!

There the book of Amos leaves the problem. Read **Amos 9** for a grim prophecy that no one can escape from the omnipresent God. The comforting verses toward the end are thought to have been added by another hand. Amos leaves us with our complacency shattered, with doom and a divine retribution sounding in our ears.

OBADIAH

---

*This unknown author's vision concerns the Edomites whom tradition
believed were the descendants of Esau, the twin brother of Jacob.
(See Genesis 25: 19–24 and p. 16.) There was longstanding enmity
between the two peoples. This reached its climax when the Babylonians attacked Jerusalem and the Edomites, so far from helping the
Israelites, did not conceal their delight.*

The writer declares that the judgment of God will fall
upon Edom for their treachery, but deliverance will eventually come to "the house of Jacob". Yet the spirit of angry
denunciation, familiar in most other prophets, is largely
absent here. There is only the conviction that God's justice
will triumph and be vindicated.

Obadiah verses 10–16
The vividness of this passage suggests that it was written while
the memory of Edom's perfidy was still fresh in the memory,
probably about 586 B.C. The closing verses of the book repeat
the refrain of most of the prophets that finally "the kingdom
shall be the Lord's" (verse 21).

JONAH

I recommend the reading of the whole of this book.

It is a great pity that one of the finest missionary parables in the world should be known to most people only as a rather impossible story about a whale. It is a famous story: everybody has heard about it, but few have got past a sense of amusement, aroused through an absurd literalism which the author certainly never intended.

The author is entirely unknown. Following a not uncommon literary custom, he fastens the fictional adventures of his hero on to an historical person who had lived 500 years before him (II Kings 14: 25). For this book was written, as we have seen (p. 60), after the Exile, probably about 300 B.C.

Of this historical person it is written that he was interested only in the growth and development of the people of Israel. Our anonymous author makes his hero the missionary who preaches a gospel which embraces all men and all nations. Here is the finest missionary message outside the New Testament.

It is amusing to recall the learned debates on whether there was a fish that could swallow a man and accommodate him for a week-end without injury. It seems to me as silly as research on The Pilgrim's Progress *to decide whether there ever was such a creature as Appollyon. Is* The Pilgrim's Progress *true? No, not literally, but "Yes", if you mean spiritually, for it is the true story of every Christian's quest.*

Similarly, is the book of Jonah true? No! Not if you mean a scientifically accurate account of actual events, but "Yes", if you mean in its profound spiritual significance.

Let us forget the historical Jonah and by "Jonah" let us understand the hero of a story.

Jonah 1: 1–3

Nineveh was the capital of the Assyrian Empire. The word means "fish-town" and we are told it took three days to cross it. Its inhabitants were the "Huns of the Ancient World". Jonah is commissioned to declare its doom and preach repentance. But Nineveh was Israel's enemy. Jonah does not want to go. It was like a minor bishop being ordered to preach in Berlin during the 1939–45 War and tell the people how wicked they were. So Jonah books for Tarshish, as far from Nineveh as he could get, possibly Tartessus in Southern Spain. He sought to flee "from the presence of the Lord". We see from this that God was still thought of as having no jurisdiction in a foreign land. At Tarshish Jonah thinks he will put the sea between himself and God, and to the Jew the sea was evil and divisive.

Jonah wanted the destruction by God of the Ninevites and he thought if he preached and they repented they would escape the judgment which Jonah hoped was coming to them. He wanted them crushed, not converted.

Jonah 1: 4–17

The dramatic story of the storm, the conclusion—superstitious to us—that the cause of it was someone in the ship, the casting of lots and the casting out of poor Jonah, who has made every ship's company dislike taking a parson on board ever since!

Jonah 2: 1–10

In Jeremiah 51: 34 Nebuchadnezzar of Babylon is likened to a dragon which has swallowed up Israel and later disgorged it. Some writers maintain that the adventures of Jonah symbolise the Exile and return of Israel.

Jonah 3: 1-10

Having reached the land, he obeys the divine call and goes to Nineveh, a city so great that it takes him three days to cross it. Perhaps the "whale" represents the city which engulfed Jonah for three days and then cast him out.

"Forty days and Nineveh shall be destroyed," he cries. And to his chagrin the people repent. Another bit of humour is often overlooked. Not only is the King converted, but he orders not only the people, but the animals to wear sackcloth! "And Jonah was angry" (4: 1). He *wanted* the people destroyed. To save them made his prophecy false and robbed Israel of the malicious joy of seeing their enemy crushed by their God.

Jonah 4: 1-11

Sulkily, Jonah goes out into the wilderness and is ready to die with pique and frustration. He welcomes the shade of a gourd and finds it next day worm-eaten and withered. That makes him angry again. The gourd ministered to *him* so he wanted it to go on living. The Ninevites were hostile to *him* so he wanted them destroyed.

Then comes the sublime climax (verses 9-11). The voice of God reproaches Jonah. He is concerned about a mere gourd which came in a night and perished in a night. What is that compared with Nineveh, that great city of 120,000 people who are only just beginning to be taught, who hardly know right from left? Why, their very cattle are more important than a withered plant! How badly out of perspective Jonah has got things! Let him rise up and see and share the love of God for a pagan people.

Remember when this story appeared. It was during a period when the official religious policy, instigated in the first place by Ezra, was rigid exclusiveness. The less Israel had to do with other peoples the better. The purpose of this policy was to preserve the true faith. But it went too far. The story of Jonah attempts to put the balance right.

The attempt very largely failed. The Jews never fully grasped their responsibility to pass on to others the truth to which God had led them. Because of this, the task of proclaiming the Christian message, which was cradled in Judaism, passed from the Jews to the "New Israel", the Church.

Jesus compared himself with Jonah (Matthew 12: 39–41, Luke 11: 29–30). He too was swallowed up in an evil world and overwhelmed by evil for three days, only to be set free by the power of God in the Resurrection to continue for ever as the Saviour of men. But the fact that Jesus quoted Jonah no more compels us to believe that the story is literal history than a modern preacher who takes an illustration from Robinson Crusoe expects us to believe in his adventures as having actually taken place.

Where the story of Jonah especially touches ours today is just here: Jonah was really angry that God loved the Ninevites. They were Israel's sworn enemy and he had declared their doom. To his dismay they repented. He wanted God to destroy them but God forgave them. God loved them.

How did we think of our enemies during the war? With what joy many people received news that some of them had been destroyed. But which does a real Christian desire most, their destruction or their salvation?

The message of the book of Jonah is that God loves all. All belong to his world family. He has set us the task of finding a way of living together.

Jonah was concerned about a gourd—careless of the lives of 120,000 people. Let us beware that we are not concerned about loss of face and prestige, about revenge and reprisal, forgetting that every life on this planet lies within the all-embracing arms of the love and care of God. Here is the strongest argument in the Old Testament that God cares about other nations beside Israel, loves their people and wills their salvation.

MICAH

---

*Unlike Isaiah, who was a man of the city, a priest and probably a
courtier, or Amos, who was a man of the desert, the wide open spaces,
Micah was a countryman, a villager we might call him, who loved
the smiling meadows and the cornfields. You can still find the chalk
hills where Micah mused about the way of God to men. At the bottom
of the glens the soil is red and fertile. Here cattle graze, birds sing,
and water flows in almost unfailing supply. The country reminds one
of Devon, and Micah has the fearlessness of the sons of Devon; men
like Raleigh and Drake and Hawkins who loved their land and
served it with independent minds, steel nerves and disciplined bodies.
He is one of the important group of eighth-century prophets.*

*In their writings, Isaiah scourged the sins of the city; Amos, the
ascetic, scourged the luxury of the aristocrats. The problem Micah
faced was that of rich, land-hungry men from the towns, buying out
the peasant proprietors and enslaving the peasants. Land that had
belonged to a family for centuries was forced out of its hands because
the peasants were starving. "They"—meaning the wealthy sharks—
"covet fields and seize them, and houses and take them away; they
oppress a man and his house, even a man and his heritage" (Micah
2 : 2 R.V.).*

*Micah realised that a townsman deprived of his trade can find
another. But in the country there are few jobs and perhaps only one
master who owns more and more of the land for miles around. The
countryman notoriously dislikes being rooted up and transplanted
elsewhere where even his peasant co-workers resent his arrival. His
alternative is to submit to a tyranny impossible in a town, but even in*

our own land in bygone years common in the countryside through the feudal system.

One might say that Micah smelled revolution and he knew that the Assyrian aggressor would welcome the inward division and strife of the people to swoop down in conquest. He knew also how terrible was an Assyrian attack, for while other invaders had slain and burned, and then gone away, the Assyrians carried whole populations into exile. How often a land is thrust into revolution by the revolt of the countrymen. It happened in the peasant rising in England in the fourteenth century. It was the prelude to the French Revolution. It was the postlude to the Reformation in Germany when the revolt of the countrymen culminated in the Peasants' War.

Micah lived at Moresheth-Gath. The name means the property of Gath, and Gath means gossip. ("Tell it not in Gath" is a characteristic Hebraism meaning "Tell it not in Tell Town, or gossip Town.") Perhaps the whole village had passed into the possession of the wealthy men of Gath. Moresheth was a village one thousand feet above the sea and, for a countryman, within walking distance of it, namely about twenty miles.

Micah is not to be belittled because of his humble origins any more than is Wordsworth because he came from humble Grasmere, or Cowper because Olney was a small village in Buckinghamshire. In some ways he is the ablest of the minor prophets, with a spiritual insight which makes part of his book of value even today, though it was written about seven hundred and twenty years before Christ was born.

I say "part of the book" because other parts, chapter I for instance, are unintelligible. This may be because the text is hard to decipher and because allusions, clear to the contemporary readers, are lost on us. Jesus was fond of this prophecy, and he quoted from it the passage about a man's principles making even the members of his family hostile to him (Micah 7: 6; Matthew 10: 35–36).

Micah saw three truths which the New Testament fills with much richer meaning and which are relevant to our lives today.

Micah 4: 1–4

1. He saw that wars between nations could not go on for

ever, depending on whichever nations happened to be stronger. Micah, as far as I can discover, was the very first to teach the theory which is now being called peaceful co-existence. Earlier teachers had regarded other nations as utterly outside God's beneficent purpose. Assyria, Egypt and the rest might be scourges in God's hand to whip Israel for her evil doings, but he was only really interested in the Jews. They were the chosen people and would vanquish their enemies and rule the world. In the meantime, the current attitude to an enemy nation was hatred. The spirit of this passage is in sharp contrast.

Slowly the world is coming to see that if life is to be worth living; if, indeed, the whole earth is not to be destroyed, fear and suspicion and hatred must give way to goodwill and understanding. God's purpose, without any doubt at all, is that all nations must learn to live together as a family. There is good, as there is bad, in all. Each has a contribution to make and each has something to learn.

Micah 6: 6–8; 18–20

2. The second truth that Micah saw was that God's love and protection cannot be bought, but only humbly accepted.

We can only imagine the daring of this countryman from the fields and meadows, who dismisses in two sentences an old system of sacrifice and blood-offering that goes back, not only to Abraham's offering of Isaac, but beyond into the earliest knowledge we possess of man's attempt to approach God. Remember the elaborate instructions in the Law as to how, and when, and by whom sacrifice was to be made to God. Imagine, if you can, man's age-long attempt to put himself right with God, to deal effectively with the problem of guilt, and then re-read this brief and beautifully worded dismissal of the whole value of blood-sacrifice.

I know that in the light of the New Testament, Micah's phrases leave a lot out. There is no talk of repentance and forgiveness. Yet though much is left out, much is said.

It is as though Micah is saying, "Religion is not the difficult and complicated thing it appears. All this emphasis on sacrifice which only a priest may offer, is unsound. You cannot get rid of your sins and find access to God like that. As long as you do the fairest and best thing you know, and add to it the mercy that prevents your actions from being merely the hard, unfeeling transaction, the soulless, loveless bargain; above all, as long as you seek the secret place of prayer and claim communion with God, then he will receive you, and you will find him." Moffatt puts it thus: "What does the Eternal ask from you but to be just and kind and live in quiet fellowship with your God?"

We do not today need to be told that a burnt offering is unnecessary. Yet there are still people who think that they must in some way buy God's attention and love. God wants a relationship of love, not a business bargain.

As the men to whom Micah spoke thought, "We would like to find what religion offers, but we must *buy* his favour with yearling calves, or rams, or oil, or the offering of our own children," so men today hold back. They think they must pass through a door of which a priest holds the key, or that they must devote money to a religious cause, or offer God time and service. They say they have not enough faith, or that they have religious difficulties.

Down the ages comes this quiet voice of a countryman saying that the heart of religion is walking humbly—the word means "in secret places"—with God. How close that is to the centre! How that gold thread runs through the Bible! So Enoch "walked with God". Abraham was the friend of God. Moses complained that he could not undertake the job because he was a poor speaker, but God said, "I will be with thy mouth". Joshua's faint heart heard the word, "Only be thou strong and very courageous . . . for the Lord thy God is *with thee*". David felt he could face the dark valley. "Yea, though I walk through the valley of the shadow of death, I will fear no evil: for thou art *with me*." And the promise goes on. Jesus, never a recluse, promises his presence—"Lo, I am *with you* all the days unto the end of the world," and he promises a Comforter, saying, "He shall be *with you* for ever."

3. The third truth that Micah saw was that God worked through his chosen leaders. Micah was among the first, if not the very first, who focussed the hopes of Israel upon a personal Redeemer.

Imagine our countryman prophesying that the Messiah should come from the insignificant village of Bethlehem, that he should be in some sense a shepherd "feeding his flock in the strength of the Lord," and adding, "And this man shall be our peace." This reference to Bethlehem was probably not simply a guess. Micah knew that David was the son of Jesse *the Bethlehemite*, and believed that from the same rustic origin the new deliverer would spring. He was to be a Saviour not from the capital, but one of themselves, one of the peasants who had been so cruelly treated, a son of the people.

I am not attracted to the interpretation of Micah's words which make them mean that Jesus would be born in Bethlehem, though I gladly recognise that the wonder of so much prophecy is that in Christ it receives a fuller implementation than the prophet could have foreseen.

I think that Micah was saying that from the birthplace of royal David, there must come another shepherd of Israel who, like David of Bethlehem, should "feed his flock in the name of the Lord". Micah sees that religion must be mediated through, and expressed in the policy of, the nation's leaders. It is not enough that those leaders should serve a party policy, let alone a personal ambition. They must be men who wait on God, real shepherds of God's sheep who are responsible to God.

NAHUM

HABAKKUK

We don't know anything about Nahum and when we are told he was an Elkoshite we still cannot identify the place. He calls his book "the burden of Nineveh" and the book certainly is weighed down with gloom and cursing.

The book is a sequel to "Jonah" and evidently Nineveh's alleged repentance has not lasted. She was again sunk in iniquity—perhaps fifty years later—and so was certain to reap the wrath of an angry Jehovah.

The Medes and Neo-Babylonians later invaded Assyria and "reduced Nineveh to ashes" (612 B.C.) so that the armies of Alexander the Great marched over the plains where it had once stood, unaware that it had ever been there.

I visited this site myself in 1918 and can speak of the desolation but not of the complete obliteration of the city. The sands of the desolate desert blow through some old ruins and certainly no one would guess at the glory of Nineveh at the height of its prosperity. Nahum would be satisfied if he could walk over the ruins of Nineveh today! But its fortunes and misfortunes are not of devotional value for us now.

I cannot find anything in this book save Chapter 1, verse 7 which I should advise the busy man to ponder.

HABAKKUK

Some may feel that this book of the prophet Habakkuk is short enough to be read right through. However, I have indicated some golden passages and omitted some cursing.

No one can tell us who Habakkuk was. It has been suggested that he held some musical position in the Temple service, but there is little evidence of this. What is clear is that, like Job, he could not square the goodness and power of God on the one hand with the evil in the world and the prosperity of evil-doers, on the other.

It has also been suggested, in the light of a commentary on the prophet found among the Dead Sea Scrolls in 1947, that the invaders against whom Habakkuk thundered were the armies of Alexander the Great. If so, the date of the book is later than 601 B.C. which used to be reckoned as the true date.

Habakkuk 1: 1–8, 12–17; 2: 1–4, 18–20; 3: 1–2, 17–19

There is a sentence of seven words in this little-read book which in particular we must not miss. In Chapter 2: 4 we read "*The just shall live by his faith*". Habakkuk then comes to the only possible conclusion concerning the problem of God's toleration of evil in the world. We can only cling by *faith* to the creed that he must be both omnipotent and loving, and decide that his love will finally be vindicated.

It was those seven words that gave Paul the basis for his argument in his letter to the Romans (see 1: 17) and we can say they undergirded, through Luther, the Protestant Reformation.

Few people singing today William Cowper's hymn beginning, "Sometimes a light surprises", realise that its closing verse is taken almost word for word from Habakkuk:

> *Though vine nor fig tree neither*
> *Their wonted fruit should bear,*
> *Though all the field should wither,*
> *Nor flocks nor herds be there,*
> *Yet, God the same abiding,*
> *His praise shall tune my voice;*
> *For, while in Him confiding,*
> *I cannot but rejoice.*

Similarly, as George Meredith sings:

> *Into the breast which gave the rose*
> *Should I with shuddering fall?*

In Habakkuk 1 : 12 God is called the Rock (R.V. margin). On that rock we must build our faith, for as our prophet said, "The earth shall be filled with the knowledge of the glory of the Lord, as the waters cover the sea" (Habakkuk 2 : 14).

ZEPHANIAH

This book is described by one commentator as "one of the most difficult in the prophetic canon". He tells us that the text is damaged and that in some passages we may be quite sure that we have not the true text; in others we cannot be sure that we have it.

I could barely find in the three chapters of this book a single sentence of comfort for my heart or food for my soul or light for my mind. We can pass on from this outburst of gloom and despondency, this prophecy of apostasy and slaughter, as having little or no message for us today.

HAGGAI

There is not much in this brief prophecy of Haggai for our time: little there is for the devotional half-hour, little for the sustenance of the spirit or the kindling of the mind. We have no notion who Haggai was save that he was a layman, not a priest.

Yet there is a kind of romance behind the bitter language. Israel has returned to its homeland after the Babylonian captivity and Haggai is eager that the people should not lapse into idleness and apathy (see p. 64 and Ezra, chapter 5).

The prophet urges the people not to attend to rebuilding their own houses only, but to repair the house of God. He stirred up "the spirit of all the remnant of the people, and they came and did work in the house of the Lord of Hosts, their God" (Haggai 1: 14). He quotes God as saying, "the desire of all nations shall come and I will fill this house with glory, saith the Lord of Hosts" (Haggai 2: 7).

In a way, this brief book marks a kind of rebirth of spiritual zeal for God on the part of Israel for whom the bitter days of captivity are over. Haggai cannot bear to think that when God has brought them through so much they should sink into slovenliness. Here is the great chance of the revival of religious enthusiasm made objective by a determination to rebuild the Temple and restore the old ceremonies and services. The people are to realise that all they have suffered has been used by God to discipline them and that now (520 B.C.) they must rebuild the Temple and reshape their own way of living. God will crown both endeavours with glorious reward.

ZECHARIAH

Zechariah is associated with Haggai in Ezra chapter 5 as urging the returned exiles to press on with the rebuilding of the Temple. But I must confess that I read and re-read the prophet Zechariah without finding much for the strengthening of my devotional life.

There are a few memorable phrases. For instance, Chapter 4: 6, "This is the word of the Lord unto Zerubbabel saying, Not by might, nor by power, but by my spirit, saith the Lord of hosts".

Zechariah 7: 8–10; 8: 16–17
Community life at its best rests on compassion and trust.

Zechariah 9: 9–10
This is the famous passage which was taken to be a prophecy of the manner of Christ's triumphant entry into Jerusalem. An important detail is that the king rides on an ass, indicating a peaceful reign, not a warhorse. In view of the hopes current at the time of Jesus that the Messiah would be a military leader delivering the nation from Roman occupation, the deliberate fulfilment of this prophecy by Jesus was very significant.

Chapter 12 verse 10 is another example of words which came to have a special link with the experience of Jesus (see

John 19: 37), and Chapter 13 verse 7 was quoted by him (Matthew 26: 31).

The scholars tell us that Chapters 1–8 contain the words of Zechariah, a contemporary of Haggai, but that the rest of the book belongs to a later period and is relevant to a different issue and written by a different hand.

The issue of the first eight chapters is the restoration of Israel, her temple and her power by means of an avenging God, and there are visions which can only be interpreted as presaging the glory of the restoration. What does come through the book is an invincible trust that God *will* restore his beloved Israel, a trust which, so far from being shattered by defeat and exile, only argues that what looks like defeat on the part of the enemy is only God's way of disciplining a rebellious people. Jerusalem *will* become the world's spiritual centre. All Jews will see the triumph of God and all Gentiles at last be drawn in (14: 9). In this way the promise to Abraham that "in thee shall all the families of the earth be blessed" would be fulfilled.

MALACHI

Malachi is an anonymous title for the editor of a number of prophecies which often have no relation to one another. The word means the "messenger" or the "angel" or perhaps better, "the angelic messenger".

The book uses, for the first time in the Bible, a kind of question-and-answer method. The author makes a statement and then writes, "But you will say . . ." Then he answers the imaginary questioner. This is a new method of Hebrew writing.

The date of the book is around 464–424 B.C. The people had returned from exile in Babylon—though some had voluntarily stayed behind for reasons of settlement in business, or marriage with a "heathen" woman—and were being well treated by their Persian viceroy.

So settled had they become that they had sunk into a complacency from which it is the intention of "Malachi" to rouse them. They had intermarried, had allowed Temple ceremonies and services to fall into disuse or, worse, had offered to God in sacrifice polluted bread and blemish-ridden animals, which they would not have dared to offer in earlier days.

In this last book of the Old Testament the priests come in for a heavy rebuke. They had become slack, allowing the Temple services and ceremonies to fall into disuse (cf. 1 : 8) and living in many cases dissolute lives themselves. Indeed, through the intermarrying which had gone on, pagan rites had crept into services in the Temple itself.

If Israel had not heeded the harsh words of her prophets, she would have ceased to be a nation. As it is, a "Day of the Lord" will dawn, terrible indeed for the wicked, but a day when God will not only reward faithful Jews but accept the worship of sincere Gentiles. This is a rare note in the Old Testament, a parallel being in the closing sentences of the book of Jonah.

Malachi 3: 13—4: 2

God will be like "a refiner's fire" (3: 1–6) and the glory of the Temple will be recovered and its worship purified.

The promise of the return of Elijah as forerunner of the Messiah (3: 1, 4: 5) has a fascination for the believer in reincarnation, but the latter cannot be proved by the words used and this is not the place to consider the evidence.[1] It might seem as though the idea was generally accepted both before and after the birth of Christ to which this book looks forward (see Matthew 3: 14).

The book closes with the heartsome message of 4: 2, "Unto you who fear my name shall the Sun of Righteousness arise with healing in his wings".

———

All the prophets seem to me to say three things clearly.

(1) God certainly is free to intervene directly in human affairs, but in fact he usually chooses to work through chosen servants, and God's people have a hand in choosing his men.

(2) Evil brings inevitable disaster to those who practise it, either in high places or in low; either at home or in councils of state. There is a law, called in the Bible the law of righteousness, and the prophets ask that that law shall be written on men's hearts, for, like all God's laws, it cannot be disregarded. As a man who ignores the law of gravity and walks

[1] See *The Christian Agnostic* (1965), pp. 207–223.

over a cliff will be destroyed in body, so will a man be destroyed in soul who disregards the law of righteousness. In neither case is it because God is vindictive, but in both cases because that is how he created the nature of things.

(3) Morality cannot long survive its divorce from religion. If the sanction and authority of God are withdrawn from morality, man will find that of himself he cannot, or lacks the initiative to, maintain it. He can continue to do justly and love mercy and practise virtue, only if he walks humbly with his God (Micah 6: 8).

As Christians we can refresh our souls by seeing all three ideas in one. Christ we regard as King of all the nations, and we feel that only in him can they find a uniting point. In companionship and fellowship with him, we find the very heart of the Christian religion, and he who came from Bethlehem is indeed the supreme clue we have to the nature of God, and the only one in whom life makes sense. He is our peace.

Where religion is central, everything else falls into a right perspective. He whose religion is only a Sunday affair proves, by the poverty of his nature and by the pagan reactions he makes to life's demands that his religion is of no real value. He worships himself, not God. But if God is really central, then our time, our pleasures, our relationships with others, our most humdrum tasks are gathered up and offered as of far more value than calves, or rams, or ten thousand rivers of oil.

> *If, at the close of day,*
> *He, resting wearied limbs, can truly say,*
> *I have walked humbly with my God this day,*
> *That is enough.*